The White Truth

The White Truth

John J. Robertson

Pacific Press Publishing Association
Mountain View, California
Oshawa, Ontario

ISBN 0-8163-0466-1

DEDICATION

To Katherine—always an inspiration

"We have nothing to fear for the future,
except as we shall forget
the way the Lord has led us, and
His teaching in our past history."
—Ellen G. White, *Life Sketches*, p. 196.

Preface

These chapters were originally lectures given on numerous occasions throughout southern California during 1980-1981 in response to questions raised in the public press and within the Seventh-day Adventist church regarding the authority of the prophetic gift of Ellen G. White. Some say this discussion has been long overdue; some are confused; many would like the picture made clearer.

My concern has been to discuss these issues as objectively as possible, focusing on these themes and not on personalities. Rather than concentrating on details, we have spoken to the broad principles which will help us resolve the problems of specific issues when they arise.

This invitation to share these thoughts with a wider audience has now come, and I welcome the opportunity to add my voice to many others who owe so much to the gift of prophecy in these last days.

—John J. Robertson

Riverside, California

CONTENTS

Preface

The Truth About Sources

My phone rang insistently. Lifting the receiver, I listened to a distressed church member excitedly ask, "Have you read yesterday's *Los Angeles Times* article[1] about controversy in the Seventh-day Adventist Church? There's a big article about Ellen G. White being charged with plagiarism by a southern California Adventist pastor. It's a big article spilled out over three pages. You ought to see it."

That by-lined *Times* story was picked up by newspapers across the nation. Church members in many places were asking and *were being asked* about this rather startling development. Adventists are not used to seeing their ministers quoted in the public press as criticizing the church they love. Headlines reading "Plagiarism Found in Prophet Books," "Did Prophet Copy Her Writings?" "Did Prophet Commit Plagiarism?" did not set well. A sense of family pride and privacy seemed violated in laundering dissent in the mass media. Too bad all that publicity had to be negative. Not a few Adventists were upset.

The *Los Angeles Times* article came at a time when other unfavorable press releases about pastoral defections were appearing in both secular and religious journals and newspapers. The cartooning and overgenerous blocks of space given to these items could not be expected to cheer most church members. On the other hand, in some cases non-Adventist friends expressed dismay and some indignation over what they thought to be distorted press coverage. Thus, some members took comfort thinking that some good might yet come from it.

The striking similarity in nearly every critical news item, whether local or national, has been dissatisfaction with the authority accorded the writings of Ellen G. White. To many, Mrs. White seems to be in their way. Some would put her on trial.

Her writings are characterized as "aberrant gospel," as "pastoral, not canonical," etc. She herself is dubbed "Saint Ellen" who needed "therapy" for her "hysteria" or "cataleptic" seizures. Her husband, as "Jimmy," is pictured as joining his wife in the writing of books in order to exploit "wealth in our pens." How sad! Obviously, some folk are unhappy with the influence Mrs. White's books still seem to possess.

Since verbal stones are being cast at her long after her death, and she cannot rise to her own defense, perhaps we can add our voice to others who have spoken in her defense. Truth has nothing to hide.

In the first place, no one should be shocked at verbal barbs directed at the authority of the writings of Ellen G. White. True prophets have never had an easy time of it either from within or from without the community of faith. In the second place, it reveals something about those who criticize. Criticism hurts, of course, and even made Jesus weep. But His pain was not of self-sympathy or even anger. It was pain for those making those accusations. Picture the Master, with tears in His voice, sadly verbalizing their own thoughts: "If we had been in the days of our fathers, we would not have been partakers with them in the blood of the prophets. Wherefore ye be witnesses unto yourselves, that ye are the children of them which killed the prophets. . . . O Jerusalem, Jerusalem." Matthew 23:30, 31, 37. A sad scene—that has been repeated often.

In fact, it was not unknown to Ellen White when she was alive. Even before the apostasy and defections of the early 1900s, her accusers were on the job. In 1868 the vigorous thirty-six-year-old editor, proofreader, business manager, and bookkeeper of the *Review and Herald* (the Adventist weekly paper), Uriah Smith, sat at his rolltop desk day after day penning answers to fifty objections to the visions which Marion Party dissenters were making.

His book, *The Visions of Mrs. E. G. White, a Manifestation of Spiritual Gifts According to the Scriptures*,[2] rolled off the clanking new Battle Creek Steam Press in 1868. On the flyleaf, under the long title, was inscribed the basic pioneer recognition of her place as a prophet in the Advent movement of Scripture. "Here are they that keep the commandments of God, and the faith of Jesus." Revelation 14:12. "For the testimony of Jesus is the spirit of prophecy." Revelation 19:10.

Then followed 144 pages answering fifty objections then raised by dissident former Adventist ministers who had formed the opposition party headquartered in Marion, Iowa. Yes, Ellen White was familiar with criticism, both polite and impolite. Other dissenters moved on stage to do their parts as her seventy years of ministry rolled on. Dudley M. Canright, John Harvey Kellogg, Alonzo T. Jones, Louis R. Conradi, Albion F. Ballenger, and others, each in turn, saw their own doctrinal viewpoints or plans being thwarted, and they lashed out.

In each situation two points emerge. One, opposition to the spirit of prophecy; two, conflict with one of the "old landmarks" endorsed by her visions. Today it is similar—like watching a rerun of an old movie. The only real difference is that the technology has changed from stereoptican, to filmstrip, to black-and-white silents, to sound-color, 3-D media.

What is the "White truth," the whole truth, and nothing but the truth about the use of sources in the spirit of prophecy books? Has some deep dark secret just been uncovered or pried loose from locked vaults and archives in Washington? Not at all.

The following statement of her son and assistant, W. C. White, made to the General Conference Council on October 30, 1911, upon publication of the new edition of *The Great Controversy*, gives the facts: "In the new edition the reader will find more than four hundred references to eighty-eight authors and authorities." (This does not mean to suggest that Ellen White directly consulted eighty-eight authors but that those authors she did consult quoted broadly from primary sources.) This same statement appeared in 1934 on page 112 in an informative little book, *The Testimony of Jesus*, by F. M. Wilcox.[3] Adventists who have read these and other books have known for a long time that Mrs. White at times employed the words of other writers in presenting the truth on which she was writing. Unfortunately many were not as aware as some have been.

But this little paragraph is not the only statement concerning her use of sources. Nor was it the first. In her Introduction to the 1888 edition of *The Great Controversy*, Mrs. White herself had acknowledged the use of two sources—divine and secular. Her primary source for her theological and historical overview was based on the visions given to her by the agency of the Holy Spirit. Unless this be granted, no one can even understand the meaning of the Introduction, let alone the authority of the book. Here is how she refers to her special Source: "Through the illumination of the Holy Spirit, the scenes of the long-continued conflict between good and evil have been opened to the writer of these pages. From time to time I have been permitted to behold the working, in different ages, of the great controversy between Christ . . . and Satan."[4]

The books of church historians and contemporary religious authors were her secondary source. Although she recognized the convenience they provided as she developed a brief condensation of church history, while quotation marks often indicate quoted materials, source references to such extracted material were generally not cited as authorities. Various historians were at times used because they could provide admirable descriptions of the events which Mrs. White wished to interpret in harmony with her primary Source of information. Her books, especially *The Great Controversy*, were not to be mere history, but an interpretation of church history that portrayed the unseen forces of good and evil working through human affairs. She wrote: "This history I have presented briefly, . . . the facts having been condensed into as little space as seemed consistent. . . . In some cases where a historian has so grouped together events . . . or has summarized details in a convenient manner, his words have been quoted; except in a few instances no specific credit has been given since the quotations are not given for the purpose of citing that writer as authority, but because his statement affords a ready and forcible presentation of the subject. In narrating the experience and views of those carrying forward the work of reform in our own time, similar use has occasionally been made of their published works."[5]

Here, then, is her acknowledgment of the use of secular and religious writers. No one should suggest that she never made such acknowledgment. Thus far, we have specific testimony from her son, William C. White, and general acknowledgment from Ellen White.

Ellen White's Introduction to *The Great Controversy* is very significant because it is the only one Mrs. White ever wrote for any of her books. The two paragraphs quoted above contain seven significant factors about her use of and views about sources: authority, authors, authorship, condensing, quoting, convenience, and brevity.

Authority. While Mrs. White cites the use of historians, she does not do so for purposes of authority. Her son stated that she referred to eighty-eight authors, directly or indirectly, in *The Great Controversy* alone. But her real Authority stands higher than all others. Simply stated, she gives supreme authority for her writings to the Holy Spirit, who caused scenes of history to pass before her in such a supernatural manner as to shed authoritative light on the meaning of those events. The converging of these two sources made possible a new kind of book—a unique book of special significance to the church and the world. Of the two sources, there can be no doubt that, in her estimation, the Authority behind the visions towered significantly above that of secular historical accounts.

Authors. Of course she used them. She had a substantial library. She was a reader. As she read and as she wrote, she was often reminded of the scenes shown her in vision: "While writing the manuscript of *Great*

16

Controversy, I was often conscious of the presence of the angels of God. And many times the scenes about which I was writing were presented to me anew in visions of the night, so that they were fresh and vivid in my mind."[6]

She not only read other authors but at times used their phraseology. She selectively incorporated their descriptions. While these authors provide some facts and illustrations the authors did not determine the conclusion or the larger perspectives reflected in her writings.

In recent years several researchers have been working to discover the extent of her use of the writings of others. It appears that in the Conflict of the Ages series especially, her selective use of other authors has been more extensive than many had heretofore realized. (The "Conflict" series includes *Patriarchs and Prophets, Prophets and Kings, The Desire of Ages, The Acts of the Apostles,* and *The Great Controversy*.)

Authorship. In the Introduction to *The Great Controversy*, Mrs. White claims credit for assembling and arranging this history of the Christian church. Anyone writing history is bound to take a point of view. A Catholic historian, for instance, will write the history of the Protestant Reformation from a different point of view than a Protestant historian. W. C. White says that his mother was guided to the history books she used in *The Great Controversy*. The probable reason is that their points of view more nearly coincided with the point of view presented to her in vision rather than the viewpoint of Catholic historians who were dealing with the same period. Thus she turned to Protestant writers because of their interest in the cause of reform, because they were familiar to readers, because the facts they dealt with were generally known and accepted,

17

and because these authors were excellent writers. What she sought were appropriate historical descriptions with which to "flesh out" the broad framework of activity that she called "the great controversy between Christ and Satan."

In writing *The Great Controversy*, considerable condensation, organization, and selection from the vast amount of material available were required to achieve a meaningful sketch of some of the major points in Christian history. Added to this was the additional task of portraying the invisible forces at work behind and within that brief historical outline. To do both demanded a special kind of authorship and insight.

She recognized and fulfilled that responsibility. She simply said, "This history I have presented." She was the author determining and "narrating" the form the book took, all the while "consistent" with her general purpose in bringing both elements together. At the same time, while under the "bidding" and superintendency of her higher Source, she could not take full credit, since she felt herself to be but the Lord's instrument or "messenger" in the process. Note her words: "Sister White is not the originator of these books. They contain the instruction that during her lifework God has been giving her. They contain the precious, comforting light that God has graciously given His servant to be given to the world."[7]

When confronted with a statement like this, you are face to face with the uniqueness of her calling. Is there not something singular in a statement like this? It is not boastful. It is simple. Yet it leads us to the heart of the matter. It leads us to divine revelation that belongs only to the prophets. She doesn't try to prove that. She simply describes it.

With this understanding of authorship, it is natural

as can be for her to make other statements even more to the point. Take, for instance, this one first published in 1882: "I do not write one article in the paper [*Review and Herald, Signs of the Times, The Youth's Instructor, etc.*] expressing merely my own ideas. They are what God has opened before me in vision— the precious rays of light shining from the throne."[8]

That's astounding! But it must be understood in the light of the totality of her work. What she had seen and what she had read blended. Not that every line was the result of a specific vision, but that out of a storehouse of many, many visions, she wrote. She reveals a sense of dedication and care as to what she says. Knowing that her readers accept her writings as from the mind of a prophet, she will be sensitive to that and will be honest to her trust. She will be aware of her calling at all times, especially when she writes for the church paper. She will select only those subjects which are compatible with the general message of her visions. Of course, occasionally there were special messages based on specific visions for particular situations. Whatever the communication, she wrote with an awareness of her commission and of the perception of her readers. She wrote as she was moved upon by the Holy Spirit.

Condensing. Her exact words on this point are, "This history I have presented *briefly*, . . . the facts having been *condensed* into as *little space* as seemed consistent." (Emphasis supplied.) This certainly suggests the free use of paraphrase, and an examination of her use of other authors confirms the practice. She drew this historical-religious material from many authors and some in particular, making it manageable for the purpose of her book. That purpose was to interpret history in harmony with the divine philosophy of history, that is, within the context of the great controversy between Christ and Satan. Although the Introduction we are considering and quoting from seems to be Ellen White's only formal statement, this condensing process may also apply to her other works dealing with the great controversy theme. In other words, she felt free to extract from other works wherever aptly stated information harmonized with what she had seen in vision, paraphrasing and condensing such extractions to fit her larger purpose.

Quoting. A casual or superficial reading of the phrases "in some cases . . . quoted" and "except in a few instances no specific credit" might, at first, seem to suggest a small number of quotations or paraphrastic summarizations. But in the context of *The Great Controversy* and similar books, it is obvious that those phrases must be understood relative to the demands of each of her books and to the vast wealth of material she selected from. In the case of *The Great Controversy* volume, it must be remembered that to compress the outstanding events in the history of the Christian church into one book would be a prodigious accomplishment. To cover this history in a portion of the book, leaving room for interpretation of that history, calls for even greater organizational skill. Understanding her task in this manner changes considerably the meaning of the phrases "in some cases" or "in some instances." They are appropriate and accurate when one considers the whole background and the tremendous effort required to compress the high points of that history into such a small compass.

For example, among the books quoted are two comparable multi-volume sets—D'Aubigné's *History of the Protestant Reformation* and Wylie's, *The History of Protestantism.* These seven volumes alone take up more than twelve inches of shelf space with their 4190 pages. *The Great Controversy*, with its 678 pages, contains only one quarter to one half of condensed, quoted, or paraphrased history. This took some doing. It would surely seem to her that she had extracted but very little from the volumes consulted. She could only use some of it and most naturally would say, therefore, "in some cases" I quoted and "in some instances" summarized.

Convenience. Mrs. White was making no attempt to write a history. For this reason she did not quote historians as "authority" for her condensations. Her purpose was not to write another history but to show the unfolding of the great controversy in the affairs of earth; thus she used reputable historians as succinctly as possible to set forth the historical framework. She used their summarized descriptions because they were presented in a "convenient" manner. How else would one go about such an ambitious project of compressing nearly 2000 years of church history? It would be natural to expect considerable paraphrasing and quoting.

These are the facts. This is the White truth about her own writings. Why not accept the explanation she gives at face value? She not only stated that she quoted and condensed from other authors—she asserted it in the Introduction. It has been published for all to read in millions of copies of *The Great Controversy* printed since 1888, the first in the five-book Conflict of the Ages series.

Brevity. You may have noted the dots in some of the above quotations. These were used to focus on the items we were discussing at that time. Now we shall supply the full phrasing to spotlight their importance. These phrases center on the concept of brevity (emphasis supplied):

"this history I have presented *briefly*"

"the *brevity* which must necessarily be observed"

"the facts having been *condensed*"

"into as *little space* as seemed consistent"

"where a historian has so *grouped together* events"

"as to afford, *in brief, a comprehensive view* of the subject"

"or has *summarized* details"[9]

All of these similar expressions are found in just two sentences! Obviously she was endeavoring, to the best of her ability, to emphasize the effort expended to compress the voluminous history of the church into such a small compass. This she and her associates did. In view of her condensing the narrative to the little space she could give to it, the words "in some instances" seem most appropriate. In comparison to what she might have used from other sources, her selection seemed as but a handful. She succeeded admirably.

Much more may be said on the foregoing factors, but constraints of space rest upon even this little book. Some observations and reflections, however, upon the significance of these seven factors are appropriate:

1. The use of the works of others need not be restricted to historians. The works of religious or inspirational authors may be legitimately employed in the same manner. Mrs. White was frank about this. In the same Introduction she wrote, "In narrating the experience and views of those carrying forward the work of reform in our own time, similar use has been made of their published works."[10]

2. It seems highly significant that this Introduction appeared in the first book printed in her Conflict set of five books. This is because the grand sweep of the

great controversy vision was among her earliest visions and became the basis for a significant portion of her writing through the years. That is, the great controversy theme was not limited to the volume entitled, *The Great Controversy,* but was the coherent principle behind a good portion of all her writings.

She had many visions on the great controversy theme besides the comprehensive 1858 vision at Lovett's Grove. That vision repeated one given ten years before. This theme appeared first in a smaller work, and later in four medium-sized volumes which served as forerunners of the Conflict series, the crowning work of her literary efforts. All five books describe the great controversy between Christ and Satan—between the two eternities. Since *The Great Controversy* was the first of this large set to be published, it is appropriate that the Introduction should appear in that volume. Although chronologically the Introduction appeared first, today it appears in the last book of the Conflict series.

3. Her sources for this Conflict series, unique in its nature, are cited in two categories in order of their importance: first, special revelation; second, church historians and religious writers. She utilized the fruits of her reading insofar as they matched (or did not conflict) with the many visions in which so many scenes of history and other subjects passed before her. Whether or not we ever know the full extent of her use of what she found in her reading does not matter. What matters is that she possessed a vast panorama of revelation by which to interpret and judge what she read. Most significantly, in this work of selecting and interpreting, she was motivated by the guiding hand of inspiration that moves upon the prophets in a very special way.

4. Her use of sources has not been withheld from her

readers. As her writings came before the general public she made this clear. Others have written of it from time to time. Why some independent researchers are shaken by what they have discovered and other researchers discovering similar facts are not disturbed is a mystery. The fact is that all this information might have been helpful instead of destructive. The more we know, the more it contributes to a better understanding of how revelation and inspiration operate. Originality does not determine the integrity of a prophetic writer. Behold and see the goodness of the Lord in graciously sending the "testimony of Jesus" to His people who are committed to keep the commandments of God! God's people have been greatly honored by the sending of His prophets in all ages. "Believe in the Lord your God, so shall ye be established; believe his prophets, so shall ye prosper." 2 Chronicles 20:20.

The Truth About Plagiarism

The question-and-answer period was lively, full of interest. People expressed appreciation for the candor and openness of the spirit of prophecy seminar. The moderator was eager to move the discussion into whatever areas the congregation felt a need. Finally, a church leader in the congregation raised his hand for the floor.

"We've heard a lot of good information today which is very helpful to us," he said, "but what we would like to learn more about is this plagiarism thing. Could you let us in on more of the facts?"

"A good question—let's do it," was the rejoinder. People there that day were not thrown off balance by the plagiarism charges. They believed there must be answers. They wanted to hear them. And answers there were.

We have already pointed out that Mrs. White herself explained in the Introduction to *The Great Controversy* her reasons for what some have considered to be a liberal use of historical and religious works in some of her books. She used resource materials from historians and religious works in developing the details of the great controversy theme. Why did she do it?

See how clearly she states "the object of this book"

in the last paragraph of her Introduction:

1. To unfold the scenes of the great controversy between truth and error;

2. To reveal the wiles of Satan, and the means by which he may be successfully resisted;

3. To present a satisfactory solution to the problem of evil;

4. To fully manifest the justice and benevolence of God;

5. And to show the holy, unchanging nature of God's law.[1]

Obviously, her purpose was not to write a history book. Her underlying purposes are here stated clearly and forthrightly. If she used other source materials to help achieve those purposes, who is to say she had no right to do it? To impose contemporary criteria on nineteenth-century authors is hardly fair or appropriate. Worse still is to imply dishonesty by using against them the heavily loaded word *plagiarism*, as understood in the modern context. Though charges of plagiarism were made by certain contemporaries, the truth is that at no time were such charges ever brought to court by any author or publisher. No suit was ever threatened. No case could have been made. In the judgment of modern copyright attorneys, she could not be judged a plagiarist, even by the more explicit standards of the 1980s.[2]

The subject of literary borrowing must be seen in full perspective as suggested by Cambridge scholar W. A. Edwards: "The practice of Homer, Sophocles, Bach, Burns and Moliere forces us to realise that borrowing may be the foundation of great art, that the mere fact of borrowing in itself tells us nothing. We must go further and ask *what use has been made of the borrowed material or method*. If we do this we shall

26

find there are many degrees of success and failure in borrowing, and that a genuine artist reveals his greatness here as everywhere else. . . .

"Without being any the less original for it, and without sacrificing his integrity, a genuine artist may borrow the *ideas*, the *themes*, the methods, and sometimes even the very *words* of others, but he must borrow imaginatively if he is to escape censure; he must have such an individual mind that all he borrows is recreated and he must weld his theft into a whole feeling which is unique, utterly different from the 'source' from which it was taken."[3]

I submit that the books in the Conflict series, without question, fulfill these criteria. I have read many biographies of Jesus but none of these volumes has ever brought me to my knees in love to Christ like the book *The Desire of Ages*. No church history has created in me a desire to be ready for "the time of trouble" or the coming of the Lord as *The Great Controversy* has. No historical documents have pulled aside the curtain permitting me to see the behind-the-scenes activity of unseen, supernatural forces impinging upon human events. Some have shown political intrigue and the machinations of men and nations, but nothing like the revelation of the play and counterplay of good and evil forces, of Christ and Satan, locked in contest for the souls of men, as in *Patriarchs and Prophets* or *Prophets and Kings*. Can anyone read the "faithful unto death" exploits in *Acts of the Apostles* and not be deeply moved to join the royal band of God's faithful witnesses?

If ever any borrowings from history, sacred or secular, have been transformed into books of surpassing inspirational beauty or welded into a coherent feeling utterly different in purpose, impact, and character from such aids, the Conflict set qualifies. They present a singular example of writing that escapes all theft charges as defined by even the strict canons used by modern copyright attorneys.

Another truth we must squarely face. It is not for us to pontificate upon how inspiration *ought* to work. Rather, we should humbly seek to learn how it *has* worked. Under the guidance of the Holy Spirit, using historical materials to declare God's purposes is not something new for prophets and apostles. Consider the following remarkable passage from Luke's gospel:

"Dear friend who loves God: Several biographies of Christ have already been written using as their source the reports circulating among us from the early disciples and other eyewitnesses. However, it occurred to me that it would be well to recheck all these documents from the first to last and after thorough investigation to pass this summary on to you, to reassure you of the truth of all you were taught." Luke 1:1-4, *The Living Bible.*

That's worth reading again and again. It is worth parsing out point by point. Luke was a Gentile convert and probably had never seen Christ. He may have seen John the revelator, who had been with the Lord and was yet alive during Luke's ministry; but we can not be sure. He no doubt learned much about the Saviour from the beloved Paul. But even Paul's firsthand knowledge of the Lord was little, if any, since he became a follower several years after His crucifixion. The Lord could have given Luke visions of Christ's life and work without his seeking other sources. Whether He did or not we do not know. What we do know is that Luke borrowed from many sources, as he himself reports.

Luke no doubt listened to the oral traditions circulating about the Saviour and checked them against the written biographies. He contacted other eyewitnesses, also. Luke checked and rechecked all of these accounts and endeavored to place them in proper sequence. His book became a consensus of recent matters of history, well-known and universally acknowledged by the Christian community, as facts which none could gainsay. Further, he grouped them together with a purpose. That purpose was to settle the believers in the "truth" they had been taught.

The whole process and purpose is strikingly similar to the E. G. White process and purpose in producing the "great controversy" story. Luke establishes the principle that inspired writers may draw upon sources other than visions from the Lord even in writing what later became the Holy Bible. They need not be restricted only to divine revelations in presenting their messages. What is true of the book of Luke is no doubt true of the other Gospels of the New Testament.

In addressing the charges of plagiarism, then, we should, first of all, not be disturbed by a prophet's use of certain aids that help to present his or her message. The inherent authority of the prophet's work rests in the divinely guided selection of materials which now form a document "unique [and] utterly different from the 'source' from which it was taken." Ellen White's introductory explanation to her writings is quite parallel to Luke's introduction to his Gospel.

In 1835, John Harris, an author whom Ellen White read and admired, and from whom she drew some material, wrote: "Suppose, for example an inspired prophet were now to appear in the church, to add a supplement to the canonical books,—what a Babel of opinions would he find existing on almost every theological subject!—and how highly probable it is that his ministry would consist, or seem to consist, in the mere selection and ratification of such of these opinions as accorded with the mind of God. Absolute originality would seem to be almost impossible. The inventive mind of man has already bodied forth speculative opinions in almost every conceivable form; forestalling and robbing the future of its fair proportion of novelties; and leaving little more, even to a divine messenger, than the office of taking some of these opinions, and impressing them with the seal of heaven."[4]

When it comes to specifics regarding legal aspects of plagiarism, it is possible to get down to the bare roots of what it was and what it was not during the seventy years of Mrs. White's ministry. It's not a matter of conjecture or opinion.

Just around the corner from my home lives a respected judge of our city. The other day I found him working in his backyard tending some fruit trees.

After a few pleasantries about avocados, oranges, peaches, etc., I asked him about the legal ramifications of plagiarism in the nineteenth century. It just happened that he had been doing some research on the topic and had a large packet of photocopies from the law library at hand. It was my lucky day! Come to the judge's backyard with me and listen to the gist of his answers to my eager questions.

Question: "What elements are needed for a judgment to be entered against a person for plagiarism?"

Answer: "This may depend to some extent on the nature of the remedy being sought [by the plaintiff]. When someone's literary production has been wrongfully appropriated by another, the owner may have an action in contract or in tort for an infringement, or an injunction against further publication of the work.

"The owner generally must show in such actions: 1. ownership of protectible property interest; 2. unauthorized copying of the material; and 3. damage to the owner from such copying."

Question: "Do you have a working definition of plagiarism?"

Answer: "Plagiarism is the wrongful appropriation and/or use of a protected literary property."

Question: "Have we always had copyright laws in the United States?"

Answer: "Yes, but not in the same sense as our present copyright laws. America adopted the Common Law of England, which included their common-law copyright. This protected the owner in the exclusive use of the production before publication, but after publication it became the property of the general public."

Question: "Did we adopt this system in our Constitution?"

Answer: "Yes. Article 1, section 8 of the Constitution gives Congress the power to promote the progress of science and useful arts by securing, for limited times, to authors and inventors, the exclusive right to their respective writings and discoveries."

Question: "Are you saying we have had two sets of laws operating side by side, then?"

Answer: "Yes, that's right. The Common Law of England is even today the law of America except where Congress or state legislatures have enacted statutes concerning the subject in question or where appellate courts have rendered a controlling decision."

Question: "What protection does common law provide against plagiarism?"

Answer: "Very little. Its concept was to protect property rights—the book or manuscript itself—until first published. There was virtually no protection after publication."

Question: "If Congress would pass a copyright law, would this supersede the common law?"

Answer: "It would. However, when Congress did enact the first copyright law in 1790, it was essentially a statutory enactment of the English common law. As courts were called upon more and more to mediate literary property disputes, Congress, in 1909, enacted the first comprehensive copyright law, and in 1976, the next major revisions were made."

Question: "Can you trace for me just how this has worked in practice?"

Answer: "The fundamental principle of the law of copyright before 1909 was that publication of the work put it in the public domain. The comprehensive 1909 copyright law established detailed procedures whereby authors could obtain the exclusive right to print, reprint, publish, copy, and vend the copyrighted work. If the author complies with procedures of the copyright law, his work is protected for twenty-eight years."

Question: "Now, I have a special reason for asking all these questions. One of our early authors in our church, Mrs. E. G. White, published many books before her death in 1915, most of which were published before 1909. She has been accused by critics of having committed plagiarism because she either quoted or paraphrased considerable amounts from many authors in these books and usually did not give credit by name to the authors whose works she used. Now, you are the judge. In your opinion would her practice have been a violation of copyright laws?"

Answer: "No, before 1909 there was virtually no law against it. Even after 1909 an injunction would have had to be sought showing that financial loss had been sustained by the author.''

Question: ''I would like to read you an explanation made by Mrs. White herself regarding her use of historians and religious writers in her day. [I read to the judge from the Introduction to the 1888 edition of *The Great Controversy*.] Would that have been enough?

Answer: ''That was adequate for that day.''

Question: ''Well, I understand she did considerable paraphrasing without specific credit. Would that have been a violation?''

Answer: ''Paraphrasing of an entire work, perhaps, but not substantial portions. That was permitted. If several works were quoted, that would generally not be a violation, especially if a major portion was independent or a new slant was given. That would be permissible. Even under the 1909 statute it was required of the plaintiff to prove three things: 1. ownership; 2. unauthorized copying; 3. damage to the owner from such copying. I do not think this could have been shown. The very fact that nobody made any claims against her is evidence that there was no case. Nobody apparently felt they were being hurt.''

Question: ''Since I presume that all the books she quoted from were from the 1800s, would that make a difference?''

Answer: ''There would be no problem there at all. In fact, most of the books that early did not even bother to obtain a copyright. They only stated the date and place of publication. Such books were in the public domain after publication.''[5]

So ended a most enlightening afternoon in my neighbor's back yard. This is information critics of those times ought to know. I have never questioned Mrs. White's integrity in the least, but it was good to hear a

33

competent and respected authority state his legal opinion that Mrs. White was not in violation of copyright laws. His verdict? Not guilty!

You may look up the word *plagiarism* in a modern dictionary and think you have an accurate definition. But if you look through the eyes of the legal profession, you do not find it to be necessarily so. If you take a historical perspective that surveys the practices of a hundred years ago or more, you do not find the practice of literary borrowing at all the same as now.

We have already examined in the Introduction to *The Great Controversy* the freshness and candor of Ellen White's own understanding of how the prophetic gift works. This volume proved to be a great blessing and a great success during its first twenty years in print. As the presses hummed through a rapid succession of printings, it became evident that the worn type would have to be reset for the new 1911 edition. It was suggested that since *The Great Controversy* was being sold not only to church members but to the general public on a large scale, the new edition should be improved with the addition of footnotes. It was felt, too, that in some places changes in wording would prevent it from being dated and would make it more acceptable to non-Adventists. When this was presented to Mrs. White, she readily assented to the suggestions and gave orders to proceed.

Her staff of regular workers, together with several invited consultants, were directed to find the exact source for each quotation and to carefully study the wording to achieve a timeless quality and to avoid needless offense to certain groups referred to. Upon completion of the tedious work, Ellen White was happy with their minor touch-ups and personally approved the changes suggested. She did not, however, make a single change on the basis that she had been unethical in her use of materials. That was never a concern. She had covered the matter of literary credits sufficiently in her Introduction over twenty years previously and would repeat it in the new edition even though in every case that could be checked, full credits were given.

From time to time, since then, some have vigorously waved the plagiarism flag, but the better we become informed of all the facts in the case the better she looks. The history surrounding the writing of her books clears the air of the negative overtones of cover-up contained in the word *plagiarism*.

One day I sat in one of our university libraries scanning the early volumes of the Seventh-day Adventist church paper, the *Review and Herald*. When I came to the year 1883, my eyes fell upon a special display ad featuring Geikie's *Life of Christ*, one of the books she had at hand while writing on the life of Christ. As I continued turning the pages in the bound volume, I discovered that this special offer of Geikie's 1256-page book, for only $1.75, had run for several months that year.[6]

Think about that for a moment. If Mrs. White were writing on the life of Christ, and if she wanted to keep all of her sources a secret, would she have used the currently advertised *Life of Christ* as one of her sources? Of course not.

My curiosity aroused, I wondered if the *Signs of the Times* might be doing something similar that year. Imagine my surprise to find a series of four-and-one-half-column-inch display ads. The headlines heralded a "Magnificent Premium Offer with *The Signs of the Times* for 1883."[7] What was this liberal offer, do you suppose? "To each new subscriber we will furnish *The Signs of the Times* one year with a copy of

Conybeare and Howson's *Life and Epistles of St. Paul*, for $2.25." Well, now, does that look like either she or her publisher was trying to cover up her use of Conybeare and Howson's book while writing her own *Sketches from the Life of Paul*, published *that very same year*? Hardly!

Further, does it seem reasonable that Mrs. White herself would join in the promotion of Conybeare and Howson's *Life and Epistles of St. Paul* in the January *Signs* of 1883 on the very eve of the publication of her book, *Sketches from the Life of Paul* if she had something to hide? Again, in the February 22 issue of the *Signs*, she writes, "*The Life of St. Paul* by Conybeare and Howson, I regard as a book of great merit, and one of rare usefulness to the earnest student of New Testament history." Some cover-up for one whose book would be published in June of that same year as a Sabbath School lesson help, wouldn't you say? The contemporary records show her as being open and above board. They vindicate her integrity. It is difficult to understand how anyone would believe she harbored any intent to deceive, a factor that is requisite to prove plagiarism.

On December 26, 1882, about a year before the fourth volume of *Spirit of Prophecy* (earlier treatment of similar material found in *The Great Controversy*) was published, she wrote the following recommendation for a set of books she was using in the writing of the chapters dealing with the Protestant Reformation: "Provide something to be read during these long winter evenings. For those who can procure it, D'Aubigne's *History of the Reformation* will be both interesting and profitable. From this work we may gain some knowledge of what has been accomplished in the past in the great work of reform."[8]

Interesting? More than interesting. Mrs. White would have to have been positively foolish to recommend books she was paraphrasing or quoting in her forthcoming books, if she hoped to keep her readers in the dark about her use of the writings of others. Plagiarism charges fall flat in the light of such facts. When the books were published, both her books and some from which she quoted were for sale side by side on the same counter in the Review office.

Publishers of the books she recommended must have been pleased at the free advertising. They would have had to agree with the practical question, "Who is harmed by it?" Certainly not they. They profited by the sharply increased sales. And, keep in mind that one requisite to plagiarism is proving financial damage. The thousands of additional copies sold could hardly be considered damage!

One further area regarding plagiarism culpability needs to be emphasized and examined. It concerns the so-called moral or ethical issue involved in citing or not citing references to sources. But we must consider a prophet's view of the sources of truth before we make hasty judgments., Readers often miss the real reason why Mrs. White seemed so unconcerned about quoting and footnoting extensively.

If you observe through apostles' and prophets' binoculars, suddenly the mind is illumined with a strikingly different viewpoint about sources. In the remainder of this chapter I would like to explore the prophet's view.

Mrs. White has stated why she felt the way she did. She said she did not give credit because the quotations she used were "not given for the purpose of citing that writer as authority."[9] That strikes me as being exactly the opposite reason for my citing an author when

I write something. The better the authority I quote, the more authoritative is my writing. Not so with Mrs. White. Her statement about "authority" is significant.

A helpful first step toward understanding a prophet's view of her work is alluded to by her son, William C. White. He provides this key: "In her early experience when she was sorely distressed over the difficulty of putting into human language the revelations of truths that had been imparted to her, she was reminded of the fact that all wisdom and knowledge comes from God and she was assured that God would bestow grace and guidance. She was told that in the reading of religious books and journals, she would find precious gems of truth expressed in acceptable language, and that she would be given help from heaven to recognize these and to separate them from the rubbish of error with which she would sometimes find them associated."[10]

This paragraph provides a crucial insight into why she did what she did in the way she did. The Lord was her Authority. She was following His instructions. We begin to see her work through her eyes. Further, there is a direct connection—with obvious verbal links—between the W. C. White statement above and the Ellen G. White statement that follows. The wording nails down solidly her view that she was following Christ's example in rescuing "gems of truth" from the "rubbish of error."[11] Look for these linking phrases in the following: "Christ did not disdain the repetition of old and familiar truths in prophecies if they would serve His purpose to inculcate ideas. He was the originator of all the ancient gems of truth. Through the work of the enemy these truths had been displaced. They had been disconnected from their true position, and placed in the framework of error. Christ's work was to readjust and establish the precious gems in the framework of truth. . . . Christ rescued them from the rubbish of error, gave them a new, vital force, and commanded them to shine as precious jewels, and stand fast forever."[12]

Did you notice that such phrases as "precious gems of truth" being rescued from "the rubbish of error" are common to both of the above paragraphs? Keep this in mind as you continue to follow Mrs. White's explanation of Christ's method of using sources. This is pivotal to understanding her rationale for "borrowing."

"Christ himself could use any of these old truths without *borrowing* in the smallest particle, for He had originated them all. He had cast them into the minds and thoughts of each generation, and when He came to our world, He rearranged and vitalized the truths which had become dead, making them more forcible for the benefit of future generations. It was Jesus Christ who had the power of rescuing the truths from rubbish, and again giving them to the world with more than their original freshness and power.

"As Christ presented these truths to minds, he broke up their accustomed train of thought as little as possible. Nevertheless a new and transforming economy of truth must be woven into their experience. He, therefore, aroused their minds by presenting truth through the agency of their familiar associations."[13]

This is a striking summary undergirding her concept of source authority. For Mrs. White, Christ is the ultimate Source of all truth, no matter where it may be found. That is the deeper reason why she did not feel concerned about citing historians as authorities. Any truth they had, had also originated with Christ.

In the light of this broader view—this prophetic

view—such statements as the following may easily be accommodated.

"I do not write one article in the paper expressing merely my own ideas. They are what God has opened before me in vision—the precious rays of light shining from the throne."[14]

The larger view emphasizes the propriety and truth of the above assertion. There is no moral turpitude, no deception, no plagiarism, and no lie. This concept is broad enough to include all the articles and books written to fulfill her divine commission, and even her letters.

We do not charge Bible writers who made liberal use of sources as being plagiarists. Not Paul—who included lines from the Greek poets; not Luke—who compiled his biography of Christ from others; not Jude—who included a verse from the pseudepigraphal Enoch. Neither can we indict Mrs. White for rescuing "gems of truth." None of these worthies was a plagiarist.

Better it is to decide on the basis of her fruitful contributions, on the test of creativity and coherency in her unfolding of biblical truths, rather than on her occasional use of uninspired sources, when concluding whether to believe or not. We shall experience spiritual life and blessing if we follow the words of the chronicler, "Believe in the Lord your God, so shall ye be established; believe his prophets, so shall ye prosper." 2 Chronicles 20:20.

The Truth About Prophets

If we believe that the Bible is inspired and is "the only unerring rule of faith and practice," why do we regard the Ellen G. White books with special respect? If the Bible is enough, why bother with any other authority? What this really gets down to is whether Mrs. White was a true prophet. We've got to settle that in order to settle the questions of respect and authority.

In a recent publication a student reporter was seeking teacher opinion about the authority of the Ellen White books. The responses reflected differing views on this basic question. One felt that her authority for the church is like that of Martin Luther for the Lutheran Church. Another considered that Paul's listing of prophets above pastors but below apostles locates her relative importance above the pastoral level.

These two views are really quite different. One view holds that Ellen White should be considered in the prophet category. The other view places her role in the pastoral category. That difference puts the finger squarely on the issue as to the nature of her authority.

In practice, it was pointed out by one view that if Mrs. White's authority as a prophet were set aside, that would be to neglect revelation and despise prophesying. The effect of doing so would damage the unity of faith promised through the ministry of the prophets as well as teachers, pastors and evangelists. Ephesians 4:11-13.

The person who advocated a pastoral role for Ellen White recognized that new attitudes regarding her role would be necessary. As for disciplinary matters, one would settle them by quoting an expert in discipline, such as a psychiatrist, rather than Ellen White. He predicted that the reactionary attitudes of some students toward Ellen White would melt away, since it would no longer be possible to clinch an argument with a "neat Ellen White quote." Her authority as a prophet would be reduced to pastoral counseling.

A third opinion was that "her writings should be used both ways"—both prophetic and pastoral. The reasoning was that since she was called to confirm the truth and correct error, this role indicated prophetic authority. And, of course, a prophet has pastoral interests while exercising prophetic authority.

What shall we think about these views? What we think determines our attitude to the original question. If the Bible is the only unerring guide, what authority shall we assign to the E. G. White books? To be more pointed, it doesn't really add one whit to the real truth, no matter what we think about her authority. She was what she was, her writings remain as her witness, regardless of what we think; otherwise *we* end up being the authority, with her writings then subject to our judgment.

So where shall we go for the answer? If we believe the Bible is "the only unerring rule of faith and practice," we must go there for information on this subject. It is not enough to say, "We have the Bible, so let's forget it." We must search for the answer to this question in Scripture.

When we turn to the Bible, we are forced to read about prophets. We come face-to-face with the question of whether or not we shall be open to accept a prophet, should one appear. Here is a "for instance." Paul writes three short punchlines to the New Testament Gentile believers in Thessalonica. They are these: "Despise not prophesyings. Prove all things; hold fast that which is good." 1 Thessalonians 5:20, 21. What are prophesyings? They are the messages of prophets. These imperatives indicate that a Christian's mind-set should not be closed toward this subject, but open. "Despise not prophesyings."

Even that is not enough. You dare not even be neutral or unconcerned. The next step must be to "prove all things." In others words, check out what the Bible prophets say about prophets so that you may know whether any claimant is true or false. Then what? "Hold fast that which is good." A positive commitment is called for when a prophet passes the test of Scripture.

The beneficial aspects of such commitment are pointed out in both Testaments. The chronicler promises gratifying results. "Believe in the Lord your God, so shall ye be established; believe his prophets, so shall ye prosper." 2 Chronicles 20:20.

This verse is a good example of an art form of Hebrew poetry known as parallelism. Each line is parallel and mutually supportive. With this in mind, look again at line one: "Believe in the Lord your God." How can one believe in God or know what to believe about God or what He wants us to do? We can't get much from nature or human reason or feelings that is authoritative. God doesn't really talk to us directly in words and sentences as He did to Adam and Eve in the garden. How then does He communicate to us? That is where line two helps us. "Believe his prophets." That's the key. This parallel construction indicates that to "believe in God" and to "believe his prophets" amount to the same thing. When God speaks in words and sentences to man today, He does so through His prophets. The word *prophet* means "one who speaks for another," or "spokesman." Prophets speak for God.

The claim of the prophets over and over in Scripture is that when they speak, it is God's word. Phrases such as the following regularly introduce the prophet's messages to the people: "Hear, O heavens, and give ear, O earth: for the Lord hath spoken." Isaiah 1:2. Isaiah tells how God spoke to him. "This vision of Isaiah" is embedded in the first sentence of his book. Isaiah obtained God's message by way of a prophetic vision—a supernatural revelation. This kind of introduction occurs frequently in the messages of the prophets to indicate authority. The ideas they speak are not merely their own. They are from God. This is special revelation at work.

In the New Testament, God speaks to man in the same way. John the revelator, in Revelation 1:1-3, tells exactly how God spoke to him. In these verses he traces the origin of his book in several steps. God gave the revelation to Christ; Christ sent it by an angel; the angel conveyed it to John the prophet, who, under the power of the Holy Spirit, wrote the book of Revelation for the people. Notice the progression in John's opening verse:

"The Revelation of *Jesus Christ,* which *God* gave unto him, to show unto his servants things which must shortly come to pass; and he sent and signified it by his *angel* unto his servant *John:* who bare record of the *word of God,* and of the testimony of Jesus Christ, and of all the things that he saw." Revelation 1:1, 2 (emphasis supplied).

Did you notice in the verse above that John calls the message of Revelation "the word of God?" That is the claim of all the prophets for their authority. They convey God's ideas in the best language they could use. Consequently, to reject the prophet's work is to reject God's word. It is that serious! On the other hand, to believe in His prophets is to believe in God—to "prosper" and "be established." It's also that wonderful!

If, then, we take the Bible as our rule of faith, we dare not reject out of hand any of His prophets. We must be open; we must "prove" and "hold fast that which is good." The Bible recommends prophets. How could the Scriptures do otherwise, since prophets wrote the Scriptures?

Some may wonder about the authority of noncanonical prophets, that is, prophets whose writings do not appear in the sacred canon of Scripture. What about that? The Bible mentions a number of prophets whose books do not appear in the Bible. More of them are mentioned in Scripture by far than those whose utterances do appear as books of Scripture. The number is about 135 to 40. What we need to know is this: How did the authority of these prophets compare with that of the prophets whose writings are in the Bible collection? Let's see what we can find.

The prophet Elisha wrote no book of the Bible. Yet he was a most powerful prophetic figure. Two astounding verses are written about his authority in Israel. For example, this astonishing account: "And he went up . . . unto Bethel. . . . There came forth two she bears out of the wood, and tare forty and two children of them." 2 Kings 2:23, 24.

This is hard to understand. Why did God let that happen? Perhaps the parents of these children were also mocking Elisha at home, and the children picked up the same disrespect. Perhaps, therefore, God removed His protecting grace. Who knows? But the fact is that rejection of the prophet is linked to the tragedy.

The other account of Elisha may be even more startling: "And it came to pass, as they were burying a man that, behold, they spied a band of men; and they cast the man into the sepulchre of Elisha: and when the man was let down, and touched the bones of Elisha, he revived, and stood up on his feet." 2 Kings 13:21.

It would be of intense interest to know more about this mysterious event. Had the dead man been a believer? Because of his past life, was he rewarded by God in this striking way? Who knows? But the fact remains—the Lord must have wanted the people to have faith in the full authority of even His dead prophet. Undoubtedly, the effect upon Israel was dramatic.

These two events together underscored that a prophet's authority should not be lightly considered. Disrespect brought death. Respect was connected to resurrection life. That is a very important spiritual fact for anyone to ponder in deciding whether to believe or disbelieve God's prophets.

But to the point at hand. No book in the Bible is called or is written by Elisha or Elijah. But each noncanonical prophet was invested with the fullness of divine authority. Consider John the Baptist. He wrote no book in the Bible. Yet Jesus said of him, "A prophet? yea, I say unto you, and more than a prophet. . . . There hath not risen a greater than John the Baptist." Matthew 11:9-11.

Several noncanonical prophets actually wrote books which have been lost. Perhaps they would have been included in the canon had they been preserved. Yet in their day they were counted as prophets with no less authority than those whose books we read. Nathan, for one, felt led of God to rebuke King David with all the authority of Elijah before King Ahab. These prophets, too, exercised prophetic authority. A list of such prophets, with their books and the biblical reference, would include:

1. The prophecy of Ahijah, the prophet—2 Chronicles 9:29

2. The Book of Gad, the prophet—1 Chronicles 29:29

3. The story of Iddo, the prophet—2 Chronicles 13:22

4. The book of Nathan, the prophet—2 Chronicles 9:29

5. The book of Shemaiah, the prophet—2 Chronicles 12:15

Another interesting and important list of prophets who were recognized fully but whose messages are not in Scripture may be added. All are women. Five are in the Old Testament: Miriam (Exodus 15:20), Deborah (Judges 4:4), Huldah (2 Kings 22:14), Noadiah (Nehemiah 6:14), and Isaiah's wife (Isaiah 8:3). And five are in the New Testament: the four daughters of Phillip (Acts 21:9), and Anna (Luke 2:36).

From all of this we may deduce that there are no first-class, second-class or third-class prophets. All genuine prophets received messages from God by supernatural revelation and served as God's mouthpieces. Whether canonical or noncanonical, it made no difference. All were prophets.

Let's do a little thinking about canonical or noncanonical writings. No canonical Scripture as we know it existed during the centuries while the books of the Bible were being written. What difference did that make? *Canon* means "rule" or "measure." Prophetical writings became the "canon," that is, the rule by which all later prophets were to be judged and all doctrine established. Obviously no canon existed until after all the Bible writers passed off the scene. It is thought that at the Council of Jamnia in A.D. 90 the Jews finally decided upon what books would be included in the Old Testament. The New Testament canon gradually came about on the basis of recognized usage by the church in the first few centuries of the Christian era. Thus, no New Testament canon existed while the New Testament books were being written.

Jerome (A.D. 342-420)—the scholar who translated the Bible into the Latin Vulgate—is generally credited with the earliest list of books of the Bible as we have them today. But even as late as Reformation times the accepted list was not absolutely fixed.

The Bible did not come floating down from the skies bound in shiny black Morocco leather, printed on India paper, with beautifully gilded edges. For much of their early history, "books" were not even bound, but were written on individual scrolls or circulated as letters. So while the problem of canonicity seems easy to us who, for a few hundred years, have taken for granted the bound copies as canonical, for those who lived in the days when the Scriptures were being written, it was an entirely different situation. How did people then know how to judge the genuineness of a prophet?

Let's go back to the first prophet of record. He was Enoch—seventh from Adam, according to Jude 14. Adam and Enoch were contemporaries. Their teachings became a basic rule by which the validity of

48

future prophetic messages might be tested.

Through the centuries, God revealed His will to more prophets. But those following Enoch had to be in harmony with the growing body of information produced by the prophets who preceded them. This is a Bible principle, as stated in 1 Corinthians 14:32: "The spirits of the prophets are subject to the prophets." That is, they must be tested by the writings of those who have been recognized as true prophets.

The Bible is a collection of what certain prophets and apostles have written and edited. The church has, under the influence of the Holy Spirit, collected these prophetical writings, sorting out the spurious from the genuine. The church eventually recognized them as a rule of faith and practice or as the canon of faith and practice. But that is all that means.

Without any question, the Adventist Church has accepted the biblical canon as official. But no church could, even if it wished to, rule out the appearance of subsequent prophets. God alone decides who are to be His prophets. "For God hath set some in the church, first apostles, secondarily prophets, thirdly teachers." See Ephesians 4:11, 12; 1 Corinthians 12:4-11, 28. People can't study to be prophets. God selects them when and where it pleases Him.

Our *Church Manual* says that one of the fundamental beliefs of Seventh-day Adventists is that "they recognize that this gift was manifested in the life and ministry of Ellen G. White."[1] Many General Conference sessions have reiterated this position by voting resolutions of confidence, affirming that the spirit of prophecy was manifested in the ministry of Ellen G. White— that Mrs. White was, in fact, a prophet.

The pioneers of the church recognized her unique spiritual gift. They searched the Scriptures and un-

49

derstood that several prophetic passages foretold the appearance of the spirit of prophecy in the "last days" just prior to our Lord's return.

The following scriptures were considered their favorites, as full and sufficient reason for expecting the gift.

The Church Legacy of Spiritual Gifts—1 Corinthians 12:28-31. The Bible lists eight spiritual gifts as a continuing heritage from the Holy Spirit. The first three in the list—apostles, prophets, and teachers—are termed "the best gifts" in verse 31. The gift of love in chapter 13 is for everyone, but of "the best gifts," chapter 14 and verse 1 singles out the gift of prophecy as being the most desirable of all. "Desire spiritual gifts, but rather that ye may prophesy." There is no record anywhere that these gifts have ever been withdrawn from the church.

The Church-Unity Function of Gifts—Ephesians 4:11-30. The gifts of apostles, prophets, evangelists, pastors, and teachers were given for the upbuilding of the church—"till we all come in the unity of the faith." Verse 13. Since this cannot be fully realized until our Saviour's return, the gifts are still needed.

Christ's Prediction of the Gift—Matthew 24. The very fact that Christ warned against the coming of false prophets as a sign of His return (vs. 24) is prophetic inference that the presence of the true gift is also probable. There cannot be a counterfeit without a genuine. Otherwise there would be no need for Christ's warning. He could have ended all expectancy by simply saying there would never be another prophet. But He didn't. He only warned against the false, which would be deceptively close to the true.

Joel's Prediction of the Gift—Joel 2:28-31. Joel states that "before the great and terrible day of the

Lord come," the gift of prophecy, including supernatural "dreams" and "visions," will be manifest among God's people. Peter referred to this at Pentecost, which he saw as a foretaste of what would take place in the last days. Acts 2:17-20. This visitation of the gift of prophecy would synchronize with wonders in the heavens: "the sun . . . turned into darkness, and the moon into blood, before the great and notable day of the Lord come" (verse 20), and "the stars shall fall from heaven" (Matthew 24:29). Many witnessed such celestial phenomena in sequence on May 19, 1780 and November 13, 1833, and recognized them as part of the larger fulfillment of Joel's prophecy concerning the restoration of the gift of prophetic visions.

Isaiah's Prediction of the Gift—Isaiah 11. Isaiah's prophecy points to the days when the Lord's return (verse 4) will be heralded to all the earth (verses 10, 11) gathering both Israel and Gentiles to the new earth (verses 6-9). Like the deliverance from Egypt to Canaan, this deliverance of the Lord's remnant the second time will be from earth to the heavenly Canaan. The pioneers noted that, according to Hosea 12:13, the prototype deliverance from Egypt was "by a prophet" and that the parallel deliverance would be similar in this respect as well. See Amos 3:7.

Malachi's Prediction of the Gift—Malachi 4. The prophecy reads, "Behold, I will send you Elijah the prophet before the coming of the great and dreadful day of the Lord." Verse 5. Jesus recognized John the Baptist's work as a primary fulfillment of the Elijah prophecy, saying, "For all the prophets and the law prophesied until John, and if ye will receive it, this is Elias, which was for to come." Matthew 11:13, 14. John was not Elijah, of course. See John 1:21. But as the Messianic forerunner preparing the way for the first advent, Christ designated his proclamation as a fulfillment of the Elijah prophecy.

That there was to be a repetition of a preparatory message before the second advent as well is suggested by the words "before the great and dreadful day of the Lord." Malachi 4:5. Pioneer Adventists assuredly did not believe Mrs. White was Elijah, but they did see her as fulfilling the requirements of a messenger who would help to organize and to guide the remnant people in proclaiming the Elijah message. This latter-day movement would prepare the way of the Lord for His second advent, just as did John and his disciples for the first. See John 1:7, 8.

John's Prediction of the Gift—Revelation 12. This prophecy takes in the whole sweep of the church in both Testaments. It pictures the first-advent expectancy of Christ (verse 2) and the anger of Satan at His birth (verse 4). It prophesies His death and resurrection. Verse 5. It also outlines a 1260 year-day period of persecution which would follow for many centuries (verses 6, 14), after which the "remnant" would appear in the last days and be recognizable by keeping God's commandments and having the testimony of Jesus Christ (verse 17). The "testimony of Jesus" is defined in chapter 1:1-3 as prophetic revelation from God and in chapter 19, verse 10, as "the spirit of prophecy."

Any one of these prophetic declarations, joined with many other references about the importance of the prophetic gift, would be sufficient reason to be open-minded and expectant toward the gift of prophecy. Taken together, the evidence for the exercise of the prophetic gift by the Holy Spirit in the last days is persuasive indeed.

The Adventist Church, on the basis of Scripture

and other preponderant evidence, has officially recognized the appearance of the prophetic gift in the life and work of Ellen G. White from the beginning of the Advent movement to the present. The current official statement of the church is clear on this point: "One of the gifts of the Holy Spirit is prophecy. This gift is an identifying mark of the remnant church and was manifested in the ministry of Ellen G. White. As the Lord's messenger, her writings are a continuing and authoritative source of truth which provide for the church comfort, guidance, instruction, and correction. They also make clear that the Bible is the standard by which all teaching and experience must be tested."[2]

The turn of the century was not a tranquil time for the church. The Kellogg problem was moving toward a point of no return. Disastrous Adventist fires had reddened the Battle Creek sky. The sanitarium burned on February 18, 1902. The Review and Herald publishing plant was destroyed by fire on December 30 of the same year. About a year earlier, Ellen G. White had warned about commercial printing of a questionable character and included an ominous sentence. "I have been almost afraid to open the *Review,* fearing to see that God has cleansed the publishing house by fire."[3]

Because the turmoil and tension within Adventist leadership involved doctrine as well as control of the denomination and institutions, a number of moves were effected that aroused much controversy. The counsel of Mrs. White was listened to closely. Battle Creek College moved to Berrien Springs, Michigan, in 1901. The General Conference and Review and Herald Publishing Association moved to Washington, D.C., in 1903. These major moves and certain doctrinal questions caused much dissatisfaction in Battle Creek, and much of it was directed toward Mrs. White. Her prophetic role was being undermined by those whose purposes were being crossed.

The matter flared into the open following a simple statement about her work made by Ellen White in the Battle Creek Tabernacle on October 1, 1904. Kellogg followers, led by the colorful, blunt A. T. Jones, exploited and distorted it. Jones said, "Sr. White herself has said publicly, 'I am not a prophet, I never made any such claim.' " In his dogmatic way he declared he had heard her say it in September of 1904 at College View, Lincoln, Nebraska, and afterward twice again in the Battle Creek Tabernacle. He then argued his point. "Now, how can you expect me in the face of this, her own publicly repeated statement, to insist to all the people that she is a prophet, and put her writings on a level with those of Jeremiah and others of the Bible? I know that she said that."[4]

You can imagine the stir that his declarations must have created. He charged on headlong: "I know that the editor of the *Review,* against her own words that she is 'not a prophet,' undertook to prove that she is one. . . . But how does the editor of the *Review* know that she is a prophet, when she says she is not?"[5]

What did Mrs. White actually say in the Tabernacle that led Jones to unleash such a barrage? Fortunately, the shorthand account of the meeting gives her exact words as follows: "I want to tell you the light has been given me, and many know what my work is. They say, She is a prophetess. I claim to be no such thing. I tell you what I want you all to know, that I am a messenger.

"I want you to know that Mrs. White does not call herself a prophetess or a leader of this people. She calls herself simply a messenger. You have listened to Mrs.

White, and you know what my testimony has been, and the same testimony has been borne to the people. I have not gone back on one sentence."[6]

Notice the difference between what Elder Jones said and what Mrs. White actually said. He quoted her as saying, "I am not a prophet." But she herself said, "Mrs. White does not *call* herself a prophetess. . . . She calls herself simply a messenger." There is a world of difference between saying, "I *am* not," and saying, "I do not *call* myself a prophet." But with Jones making inflammatory speeches in a divided Battle Creek, presenting his own version of what she said, consternation continued. The fact is that nowhere, at any time, did Mrs. White use Jones' words, "I am not a prophet."

To quiet the turmoil, it became necessary for Mrs. White to address the matter directly. She did so almost four months later: "I said that I did not claim to be a prophetess. I have not stood before the people claiming this title, though many called me thus. I have been instructed to say, 'I am God's messenger.' . . . With pen and voice I am to bear the messages given me."[7]

She wrote a letter to Elder O. A. Olsen four days later, explaining further about the sorry misunderstanding. "During the discourse I said that I did not claim to be a prophetess. Some were surprised at this statement, and as much is being said in regard to it, I will make an explanation. Others have called me a prophetess, but I have never assumed the title. I have not felt it was my duty to thus designate myself. Those who boldly assume that they are prophets in this day are often a reproach to the cause of Christ.

"My work includes much more than this name signifies. I regard myself a messenger entrusted by the Lord with messages for His people."[8]

Because the agitation continued, the General Conference Committee eventually published a lengthy statement of nearly 100 pages entitled, "A Statement Refuting the Charges Made by A. T. Jones Against the Spirit of Prophecy and the Plan of Organization of the Seventh-day Adventist Organization." It dealt with Mrs. White's Battle Creek statement and other charges against her. The date of publication was May 1906, or twenty-two months after the tabernacle statement. So the contrived incident turned out to be a rather lengthy interlude.

Though Mrs. White did not wish to use the title or make the claim during the entire episode, for the reasons stated, she finally found it necessary to be more categorical about it. These two statements were eventually made in 1906. " To claim to be a prophetess is something I have never done. If others call me by that name, I have no controversy with them. But my work has covered so many lines that I cannot call myself other than a messenger, sent to bear a message from the Lord to His people and to take up work in any line that He points out."[9] "My commission embraces the work of a prophet, but it does not end there."[10]

To summarize, Mrs. White gave three reasons why she did not use the title *prophet:* (1) because her work included more than the word *prophet* usually means, not less; (2) because some who claimed it were a reproach to the cause of Christ; (3) because the Lord instructed her to use the term "messenger" as being more comprehensive and less offensive.

No doubt should persist as to whether Ellen White considered herself a prophet. Although she preferred the term "messenger" as being more comprehensive and less controversial, the term "messenger" should cause no confusion as to her self-understanding. Indeed, it is the same term by which Malachi described the work of the prophet John the Baptist. "I will send my messenger, and he shall prepare the way before me." Malachi 3:1. Jesus, too, used it in referring to John. "But what went ye out for to see? A prophet? yea, I say unto you, and more than a prophet. For this is he of whom it is written, Behold, I send my messenger." Matthew 11:10, 11. It is interesting that Heaven has designated this term of "messenger" for both the prophet who prepared the way for Christ's first advent and for the one called to prepare the way for His second advent. John made no claims to the term. Although John said he was only a "voice," Jesus called him a prophet. Ellen White made no claims. She said she was the Lord's messenger.

Some have also puzzled over another term by which she characterized her writings. She wrote: "The Lord has given a lesser light to lead men and women to the greater light."[11] What does this term mean?

This self-understanding also finds a counterpart in the experiences of John the Baptist. He was awed by the object of his mission as the forerunner of the Messiah. He was anxious that his position not get in the way of the one to whom his gospel pointed. When the spotlight of attention and curiosity fell upon him, especially in regard to who he was, he deflected such questions by pointing the people to Him "whose shoe's latchet I am not worthy to unloose." John 1:27. Later, when Christ's public ministry began and John's supporters again were concerned about his position, he said, "He must increase, but I must decrease," John 3:30. John's joy was fulfilled in preaching Christ.

Mrs. White, too, was consumed with her mission to exalt the lovely Jesus and to make plain the Scriptures which pointed to the One who was coming again.

The focus of her work was on the future and final events of the great controversy. Her great purpose was to prepare the way of the Lord. She wanted no spotlight to fall upon her as a person but on the Scriptures, exalting Christ. Therefore she turned from a discussion of her position by characterizing her work as the lesser light leading to the greater light of Scripture. She declared in her Introduction to *The Great Controversy*: "The Spirit was not given—nor can it ever be bestowed—to supersede the Bible; for the Scriptures explicitly state that the word of God is the standard by which all teaching and experience must be tested."[12]

But her understanding of her role as a "lesser light" in no way diminishes her function as God's messenger, any more than John's characterizations of his work and position minimized his role.

At the Bureau of Standards our government has established official weights and measures. Here are the standards by which all weight scales and tape measures are tested. When a scale or a ruler passes the test of the original, it, too, is accepted as genuine. Still, the official standard remains the standard by which all others must be judged. In a sense, the standard remains the greater and all others lesser. The original standard remains official even though in fact all true weights and measures are exactly the same as the official standard.

Similarly, the Christian community has agreed to a standard of faith and practice in the prophetic writings. We believe God has superintended that collection, called the canon. We agree that it is our official rule of faith, not because we have agreed to it, but because of its Source. When a prophet appears who passes the test of the standard for prophets, that prophet must be accepted as genuine. Still, the official standard remains the standard. Thereby, it remains the greater authority even though, in fact, all true prophets through the ages have been lesser lights compared to the growing standard of faith and practice established by the prophets before them. Prophets are prophets, or else they are not prophets at all. There are no halfway prophets.

The Truth About Authority

The reason why the authority of Ellen White's writings is questioned is because we are faced with extrabiblical authority. Because the Seventh-day Adventist Church, and Mrs. White herself, insist that the Bible and the Bible alone is the rule of faith and practice, the question of her authority cannot be avoided.

One man put it this way: "She seems to tell us on the one hand to cling to our Bibles and then to say on the other, 'The Bible only—but you had better accept my interpretation.' "

But could her authority be less than that of a prophet and she still be a prophet? Could an inch be less than an inch and still be an inch?

Any claim that Ellen White's writings carry no teaching authority must fly in the face of her own statements. As we have seen, she declares unequivocally, "My commission embraces that of a prophet, but it does not end there." She either told the truth or she didn't. If she didn't, what further confidence could we have in her even if she honestly but mistakenly thought so?

Furthermore, any one who suggests that Ellen White's teaching authority ended at her death will have to direct the same question to biblical prophets. Did any prophet, or did any of their contemporaries, ever suggest that the authority of the prophet's message would be diminished at his or her passing? In respect to Ellen White, she spoke to this issue in 1907: "Whether or not my life is spared, my writings will constantly speak, and their work will go forward as long as time shall last. My writings are kept on file in the office, and even though I should not live, these words that have been given to me by the Lord will still have life and will speak to the people."[1]

The ramifications of this problem are far more serious than the outcome of a simple parlor game. The influence of the spirit of prophecy is woven into the warp and woof of Adventist faith, life, and organization. Largely through her influence the Adventist Church has been preserved from doctrinal disunity, after the manner of fragmented Protestantism. What we are as a church is a reflection of our faith in the divine authority evident in the writings of Ellen G. White.

The worldwide fellowship of the Seventh-day Adventist Church today, living out certain values in faith and work, is not the result of some doctrinal myth developed in recent decades. The influence of the prophetic gift was very strong among us from the very beginning. That the "little flock," beginning with such distinctively different doctrines and standards, could be welded into a solid unit is truly a marvel. No less remarkable is that this movement has demonstrated such broad appeal to so many nations, tribes, and peoples and has grown into a worldwide fellowship without national schism. This markedly demonstrates the dynamic of the Holy Spirit's authority working through the gift of prophecy. None of this can be attributed to the power of a developing myth.

The church's danger is not—as some say—in recognizing the authority of Ellen White's literature in doctrinal matters but in ignoring our past history. Moses' farewell message before relinquishing prophetic leadership to Joshua has a contemporary ring. His plea was, "Only take heed to thyself, and keep thy soul diligently, lest thou forget the things which thine eyes have seen, and lest they depart from thy heart all the days of thy life: but teach them thy sons, and thy sons' sons." Deuteronomy 4:9. In the church's march toward the heavenly Canaan similar overtones vibrate in these words: "We have nothing to fear for the future, except as we shall forget the way the Lord had led us, *and His teaching* in our past history."[2]

The authority of Ellen White's messages is no less seen in His "teaching in our past history," than it has been in the way "the Lord has led us." The uniqueness of Adventist teaching resides in the "old landmarks," which generally include the distinctive doctrines regarding the sanctuary, second coming, three angels' messages, nature of man, the seventh-day Sabbath, and the millennium.[3] Mrs. White's role in their formulation demonstrates the nature of her prophetic authority.[4]

In the development of these "landmarks," Mrs. White's authoritative role is unquestioned. Mrs. White reminisced about those early days when these distinctive doctrines were established: "One error after another pressed upon us; ministers and doctors brought in new doctrines. We would search the Scriptures with much prayer, and the Holy Spirit would bring the truth to our minds. Sometimes whole nights would be devoted to searching the Scriptures and earnestly asking God for guidance. Companies of devoted men and women assembled for this purpose. The power of God would come upon me, and I was able to clearly define what is truth and what is error."[5]

Her doctrinal authority was asserted *after diligent Bible study*, at the point of defining what was truth and what was error in the group's several conclusions. Her phrase "power of God" described more than simply a feeling or an impression as to whether or not the doctrines being studied were valid. Notice further: "As the points of our faith were thus established, our feet were placed upon a solid foundation. We accepted the truth point by point, under the demonstration of the Holy Spirit. I would be taken off in vision, and *explanations would be given me*."[6] The following sentence illuminates her function even further: "It [light] has been given to correct specious errors and to specify what is truth."[7] She refers to "every pin and pillar of the faith" as that "established by the word of God and by the revelations of His Spirit."[8]

How, then, can such authority be reconciled with Mrs. White's own stated position that the Bible is our only rule of faith and doctrine? Some today feel that this position is inconsistent with the statements quoted above. They see a danger of two competing authorities. Consequently, they would limit her authority to matters of pastoral concern and homiletical teaching. Some would rank her gift above pastors but below apostles and Bible prophets. Others would say she was a dear little lady who was sincerely mistaken about the nature of her inspiration. Still others would maintain that what she thought were visions, in fact, were but hallucinations or cataleptic seizures.

A common denominator seems to emerge. Such views consider her to be something less than a prophet with doctrinal authority—enough less so that each person is free to determine his own interpretation of Scripture. Thus one's own authority may compete with the gift of prophecy.

But it is not necessary to limit the messenger's authority in order to keep the Bible first. Once it is accepted that Ellen White was a prophet, would it not follow that harmony would exist between the teachings of biblical prophets and her own? She offers nothing that contradicts biblical doctrine. She offers no new rule of faith. Why then should her writings and the Bible not be in harmony? Her stated role is to exalt the Scriptures, not to compete with them. Perhaps the real need to be addressed is that of discovering the harmony between the two sources.

Consider for a moment how many prophets have functioned in the past. Did any legitimate prophet disagree with those who had gone before? That is the genius of the Book of Books. An underlying harmony is evident from Genesis to Revelation. What authority would remain for any prophet if all disagreed with one another on rules of faith and doctrine? Because they speak for God and do not merely air their private opinions, they can all speak with one voice in doctrinal matters.

Mrs. White is consistent in understanding her role in relation to Scripture. What she says so directly and simply is what a genuine prophet who believes the Bible ought to say. "The Bible must be your counselor. Study it and the testimonies God has given; for they never contradict His Word."[9] "If the *Testimonies* speak not according to this word of God, reject them. Christ and Belial cannot be united."[10] That, it seems, is the only logical solution. That is the White truth about authority.

But what if it seems that the testimonies contradict

the Bible? If you feel sure of that, reject them. On the other hand, *how can you be so sure you are sure?* To what extent may the difficulty be in your interpretation of the Bible which you put up against light cast on the point by messages from God through His messenger? The problem could be with your understanding and not with the gift. Even if you are sincerely wrong but think you are right, Mrs. White's advice is to go to the Bible and cling to it. She had no question as to the result of such study. With her characteristic directness and simplicity, devoid of the special language of theology, she lays it on the line: "How can the Lord bless those who manifest a spirit of 'I don't care,' a spirit which leads them to walk contrary to the light which the Lord has given them? But I do not ask you to take my words. Lay Sister White to one side. Do not quote my words again as long as you live until you can obey the Bible. When you make the Bible your food, your meat, and your drink, when you make its principles the elements of your character, you will know better how to receive counsel from God. I exalt the precious Word before you today."[11]

It would not hurt to hold in abeyance for a while those things that may seem unclear or contradictory. We do this with the Bible. Nowhere is it promised that every problem will be removed. We may have to live with some things hard to understand. Ellen White stated it clearly: "God does not propose to remove all occasion for unbelief. He gives evidence, which must be carefully investigated with a humble mind and teachable spirit, and all should decide from the weight of evidence."[12]

Ellen White did not feel it her responsibility *to make* church members believe her messages. But she apparently did feel a responsibility to tell it as it was. On the

5—T.W.T

truth itself she never waffled. She was never in doubt.

Of the pillars distinctive to Adventist faith she wrote in 1905: "When the power of God testifies as to what is truth, that truth is to stand forever as the truth. No after suppositions contrary to the light God has given are to be entertained. . . . The truth for this time, God has given as a foundation for our faith. He Himself has taught us what is truth. . . .

"We are not to receive the words of those who come with a message that contradicts the special points of our faith. . . . And while the Scriptures are God's word, and are to be respected, the application of them, if such application moves one pillar from the foundation that God has sustained these fifty years, it is a great mistake." [13]

Every organization—even of five little boys who build a little shack and form their own clubhouse—has the right to make its own rules for membership. The church in general session has for scores of years defined its doctrinal positions and published them in its official manual. Some things will have to stand if we are to maintain our integrity and uniqueness. The old landmarks are such centralities. Hundreds of thousands continue to find in our distinctive points of faith that which meets their deepest needs—certainty, freedom, new life, and deliverance.

Of necessity, certain truths are clarified by prophets. This does not imply that study should cease. Truth advances. There is plenty of room for further study. But the Bible itself offers abundant evidence that advancing light does not contradict past light. What was truth in Abraham's day did not become error in Christ's day.

With the writings of Ellen White, as with the Bible, time and place must be considered. We do not need to wear high-buttoned shoes. Old truths can afford new dress—new ways of presentation. A seminary professor—one of the venerable ancients—told a story on himself that illustrates the point beautifully. He said that, as a conscientious student many years before, he had read in an E. G. White book that most people eat far too much. Being both conscientious and short of cash, he thought it a good idea to cut his rations by one fifth. He then reported, "I did that, and was getting along quite well for several weeks. Then one day I happened to read that same sentence again. It read exactly the same as before. Being conscientious and still short of money, I cut my rations another 20 percent! That was harder, and I began losing weight and was getting weak. I read the sentence again, and it finally dawned on me that I would have to use my head!" Yes, time and place must be considered.

There is no excuse for not using one's head. Surely there are areas where certain applications of truth become an individual responsibility between oneself and the Lord. In addition, seeing truth is a growing experience. None of us sees the whole picture at once, and we are responsible for only what we see at the moment.

In areas of individual application where the church has not been explicit there is great need to avoid sitting in the judgment seat. It pays to be strict with oneself and tolerant of others. Let God be God. As Paul wrote, "Forbearing one another in love; endeavoring to keep the unity of the Spirit in the bond of peace." Ephesians 4:2, 3. That would be good counsel to remember even in discussing doctrinal centralities, for that matter.

The year 1905 was not a happy year for the Adventist Church. John Harvey Kellogg's book, *The*

Living Temple, had been published in 1903; and a number of ministers, doctors, and professors in Battle Creek were as bright lights about to go out. Battle Creek was in ferment over the heresy and implications of Kellogg's book and Ellen White's counsel regarding the future of the medical work in Battle Creek.

From England blew another contrary wind of doctrine attacking one of the old landmarks. The sanctuary truth was being challenged by the pen and voice of Elder A. F. Ballenger, an attractive man of pleasing address. His tendency was to develop a line of thought by reading into passages such detail that they effectively lost their original intent. Mrs. White characterized his method as "spinning out theories that are not sustained in the Bible."[14]

When the General Conference met that year in Washington, Ellen White, in several interviews with Ballenger and in subsequent letters, endeavored to point out his errors. But Ballenger rejected her counsel and continued preaching against a two-apartment ministry of Christ in the heavenly sanctuary.

In a series of letters from 1905-1907 Mrs. White not only pleaded with him personally but pointed out the seriousness of tampering with one of the central pillars of truth. She met the issue squarely. In this action Mrs. White demonstrated, at once, both her pastoral concern for this faltering pastor and her prophetic authority in correcting error and confirming truth. Extracts from the E. G. White letters concerning Ballenger are revealing. Here we see reconfirmed the truth that additional light cannot mean contradiction of the "waymarks." She wrote: "For the past fifty years every phase of heresy has been brought to bear upon us . . . especially concerning the ministration of Christ in the heavenly sanctuary. . . . But the waymarks which have made us what we are, are to be preserved as God has signified through his word, and through the testimony of his spirit."[15]

Notice here the parallel testimony of the Bible and the spirit of prophecy in bringing the movement to its understanding of the sanctuary doctrine. The authoritative nature of the old landmarks is God-signified through both the Bible prophets and Ellen White writings. That is strong and plain language. Later she wrote this: "As the great pillars of our faith have been presented, the Holy Spirit has borne witness to them, and especially is this so regarding the truths of the sanctuary question. . . . In vision I was given such a view of the heavenly sanctuary, and the ministration connected with the holy place, that for many days I could not speak of it."[16]

In a letter to a Ballenger supporter, Ellen White counselled: "You have helped in confusing the understanding of our people. The correct understanding of the ministration of the heavenly sanctuary, is the foundation of our faith."[17]

Just how insistent Ellen White was that new light must not alter an old landmark truth, the following strongly worded statements regarding Ballenger's position illustrate: "We are not to receive the words of those who come with a message that contradicts the special points of our faith.

"Elder Ballenger's proofs are not reliable. If received, they would destroy the faith of God's people in the truth that has made us what we are. We must be decided on this subject: for the points that he is trying to prove by Scripture are not sound.

"God never contradicts himself. . . . Another and still another will arise, and bring in supposedly great light, and make their assertions. But we stand by the old landmarks."[18]

"The truths given us after the passing of the time in 1844 are just as certain and unchangeable as when the Lord gave them to us in answer to our urgent prayers. The visions that the Lord has given me are so remarkable that we know what we have accepted is the truth. This was demonstrated by the Holy Spirit. Light, precious light from God, established the main points of our faith as we hold them today.

"I know that the sanctuary question stands in righteousness and truth just as we have held it for so many years.

". . . We know that Brother Ballenger's position is not according to the word of God."[19]

These excerpts make abundantly clear that Mrs. White considered her visions as from heaven—fully authoritative and fully supportive of Scripture. She viewed all the old landmark doctrines in this light and especially emphasized the sanctuary doctrine then under attack. She was solid and immovable in her assertions that her visions and the teaching of Scripture were in total harmony. Ballenger's denial of a first-apartment ministry of Christ in the heavenly sanctuary with all its implications was particularly singled out as error. No way was left open to accept Mrs. White as a prophetic voice on the one hand and Ballenger's theory contradicting a landmark doctrine on the other. This was not simply because to do so would be contrary to the authority of the spirit of prophecy, but because it would be contrary to the authority of both the Bible and the spirit of prophecy.

These practical lessons of history make clear the proper relationship between Scripture and the writings of Ellen White.

As a position of fact, the church—indeed Mrs.

White—asserts that we "maintain the Bible, and the Bible only, as the standard of all doctrines," in contrast to "the opinions of learned men" and "decisions of ecclesiastical councils."[20] This means sound biblical exegesis and scholarship. It also allows for theological investigation. At this level the spirit of prophecy provides both direction and correction. The conclusions of valid theologizing will not negate the theology of the prophets.

Prophets do not, by and large, engage in various forms of biblical exegesis, scholarly investigation, and systematic theology. The Bible itself is not a systematic theology. At the same time, the writings of the prophets are the stuff of which theology is made. Although all agree that Mrs. White is not part of the accepted canon she is, nevertheless, a prophet. As such her role has to be significant. In formulating a biblical theology, we must not ignore her authoritative role in arriving at correct conclusions. Perhaps her function is similar to that of a level, square, and plumbline in this matter of assembling the building materials of Scripture into doctrine or theology.

Due caution is necessary, however, in making sure that our eyes remain on Scripture. One purpose of the spirit of prophecy is to point us to Scripture and increase our appreciation for it. The prophetic gift can provide insights, correctives, and incentives to biblical study. It can "correct specious errors" and "specify what is truth . . . saying, 'This is the way, walk ye in it.' "[21] But from the Bible itself we must be able to give reasons for the hope that is in us. The gift of prophecy fails in its objective if we become giants in the spirit of prophecy and pygmies in Scripture.

In saying this, we are not ignoring the square, level, and plumbline. The two sources fit together. It doesn't make sense to disregard the prophetic gift. If we believe that Ellen White was truly inspired, we stand on vantage ground. If we properly do sound Ellen White exegesis, as we do biblical exegesis, we may safely do our theological work today. After all, doctrinal disunity in Christianity generally has not been avoided even though theologians have had modern exegetical tools at their command.

One should not ignore a prophet's authority in doctrinal concerns, whether the prophet be canonical or noncanonical. The theological messages of such noncanonical prophets as Elijah, Micaiah, Azariah, Huldah, Nathan, Gad, Shemiah, Iddo, and Ahijah were authoritative. The Bible makes no distinction between their doctrinal authority and the authority of Haggai, Zephaniah, or Habakkuk.

As a prophet, Mrs. White conveyed the Lord's messages, not her own. Only in this capacity could she give this advice: "Study it [the Bible] and the testimonies God has given; for they never contradict His Word."[22]

Only as she was shown clear explanations of truth would she have the right to correct error of human devising or confirm truth as developed in valid Bible study. The authoritative role of Ellen G. White rested on her consistent support of biblical authority and her faithfulness to the biblical norm. Anything less would be denial of her prophetic authority. Anything more would be usurpation of scriptural authority. If one could not conscientiously agree with Ellen White's statements on doctrine, such disagreement would seem to constitute a de facto rejection of her claim to prophetic authority.

Reviewing the actions and words of Adventist pioneer leaders, one discovers how they understood the nature of spirit of prophecy authority. Who, for example, can imagine a rugged nineteenth-century individualist like Joseph Bates agreeing to set aside his six o'clock "even to even" Sabbath observance unless he believed in the authority of an Ellen White vision? The record is that "this settled the matter with Brother Bates, and general harmony has since prevailed among us upon this point."[23]

It would be flippant to say that those early pioneers were mindless manikins so manipulated by a young, uneducated girl's visions that when she spoke they yielded their opinions automatically or that they put their minds in neutral. J. N. Loughborough's explanation is far more likely: "The reason these persons gave up their differences was not simply because Mrs. White said they must give them up, but because in the same visions they were pointed to plain statements of Scripture that refuted their false theories, and had presented before them in contrast a straight and harmonious track of Bible truth."[24]

At the same time, other evidences of her special role as the Lord's messenger became convincing. All these evidences could not be ignored.

J. N. Andrews, in his characteristic, orderly way, addressed the authority issue in an article entitled "Our Use of the Visions of Sr. White." He wrote: "*1 Cor. 12 and Eph. 4*, which define the gifts of the Spirit of God, *cannot really form a part of the rule of life of those who affirm that the Scriptures are so sufficient in themselves that the gifts of the Spirit are unnecessary.* . . . While the Bible recognizes the gifts of the Spirit, these are not given to supersede the Bible nor yet to fill the same place as the Bible. . . *They also constitute the means whereby God preserves* his people from confusion by pointing out errors, *by correcting false interpretations of the Scriptures, and causing light to shine*

*out upon that which is in danger of being wrongly un-
derstood*, and therefore of being the cause of evil and
division to the people of God. In short, their work is to
unite the people of God in the same mind and in the
same judgment *upon the meaning of the Scriptures.
Mere human judgment, with no direct instruction from
Heaven, can never search out hidden iniquity*, nor ad-
just dark and complicated church difficulties, *nor prevent different and conflicting interpretations of the
Scriptures.* It would be sad indeed if God could not still
converse with his people.''[25]

Ellen White's special role must be seen in tandem
with and in support of Scripture. The fact that "the
spirit of prophecy" is a term descriptive of the work of
all prophets makes this necessary. Unless this were so,
her ministry could not meet the conditions of the book
of Revelation, chapters 1:1-3; 12:17; and 19:10.

Adventist writers have dealt with this fact through
the years. George I. Butler described the natural relationship: "We do not hold them to be superior to the
Bible, *or in one sense equal to it.* The Scriptures are
our rule to test everything by, the visions as well as
other things. That rule, therefore, is of the highest
authority; the standard is higher than the thing tested
by it. If the Bible would show the visions were not in
harmony with it, the Bible would stand, and the visions
would be given up.''[26]

Another fact should be kept in mind. Mrs. White
never claimed infallibility. In fact, she disclaimed it:
"In regard to infallibility, I have never claimed it; God
alone is infallible.''[27] Our writers have cautioned
against jot-and-tittle perfection. F. M. Wilcox wrote:
"The work of Mrs. White should not be judged by
some detail, by the turn of a phrase or a sentence, or by
some seeming contradiction in her writings. It should

74

be judged by the spirit which characterized her work through the years, by the fruit it has borne in connection with the great religious movement with which it was associated, and in the development of which it bore a prominent part and exerted a molding influence."[28]

Reflecting upon the evidence, there can be no doubt but that the authority of Ellen White has been substantial. We are confronted by two stoutly affirmed and parallel positions. First, it is the stated position of both the church and Mrs. White that the Bible alone is the rule of faith and practice. Even the authenticity of the messenger must be judged by it. Second, both church teaching and the evidence of her own writings affirm that Ellen White was a prophet. As such, her role was to magnify Scripture, correct error, and confirm truth.

However, if a seeming variation in content is perceived, the question of relative authority between Scripture and the gift of prophecy may arise. Several factors may contribute to faulty perceptions, resulting in the conclusion that the two sources are in contradiction.

Ellen White advised: "Regarding the testimonies, nothing is to be ignored; nothing is cast aside; but time and place must be considered."[29] Basic principles underlying counsels that may seem outdated must be sought out, whether recorded in her writings or in Scripture. In addition, it is wise to weigh all the references on any given subject to find balancing statements.

Another factor of which we must be aware is the package of presuppositions and backgrounds each reader brings to a particular passage. One of the strange realities of life is that two persons can compile passages seemingly to support opposing views from either the Bible or the spirit of prophecy. This should prompt the student of the Word to look for the higher theological principle that unites what seems to be conflict rather than to develop a theology of paradoxes or, worse, contradictions.

In summary, if we grant that both scriptural prophets and the modern manifestation of the gift are genuine manifestations from the same Spirit, there must be underlying harmony without contradictions. If anyone thinks he sees a problem in Ellen White's writings, he should keep in mind that apparent problems arise even within the Scriptures themselves. We often need to patiently hold some problems in abeyance until more information is available. One should not allow one point to fester until it distorts appreciation for the whole. Furthermore, since spiritual things are spiritually discerned, mere scholarship may not solve every problem. If we listen to the Spirit that inspires prophetic writings, we shall become wise unto salvation. Was that why John said so many times, "He that hath an ear, let him hear what the Spirit saith unto the churches"?

The Truth About
Inspiration and Revelation

"What are we supposed to do now since we know that some of the familiar quotations in the E. G. White books were originally set forth in the words of someone else?" people have recently asked.

If you want a short, short answer, it could be, "You don't need to do anything. Truth is truth no matter who expressed it first." That would make this the shortest chapter in this little book—it would end right here.

But to be more helpful, we need to probe more deeply into the principles of inspiration and revelation. If you have read chapter 2 on plagiarism, you have seen that Bible writers at various points include material from other sources. Yet we consider such passages to be as much a part of the Word of God as any other. Jesus, John, Jude, and many others included the sayings of others as part of their messages, which are now part of the Bible.

Early in her ministry, Mrs. White, concerned about her lack of experience as a writer, was instructed that in the reading of journals and books she would find "gems of truth" sometimes together with the "rubbish of error." She would be given wisdom to recognize the "gems" and to use them for her messages. Out of this we may recognize a principle of inspiration at work: The Holy Spirit guides the prophets in recognition of truth.

Another principle of inspiration we have seen is that all "gems of truth," wherever found, have Christ as their Author and Source. Hence, the self-same Spirit who revealed "gems of truth" to an earlier writer inspires the later prophet to recognize it anew. We may even go a step further and say that as we read the truth the prophet has set forth, the self-same Spirit will, if our hearts are open, reveal to us its beauty in a way that will change our lives.

While "truth is truth wherever it is found," yet in God's lovingkindness the marvelous "spirit of prophecy" body of writings penned by all of His prophets, serves as a norm against which to test all subsequent prophetic writings. This also is a principle of inspiration: "The spirits of the prophets are subject to the prophets." 1 Corinthians 14:34. This is why Mrs. White's teachings must pass the test of Scripture, too, even as Paul recognized his writings must.

But this does not mean, though, that you and I are inspired because we may say something that agrees with the Bible. Because we are really talking about how prophets operate, we must discover how their inspiration is different from ours. We often say that we are inspired when we hear a sermon, see the majesty of craggy snow-capped peaks, hear sublime music, or look into a baby's face. That is what may be called *general* inspiration. God's voice may speak in this way through nature.

Then we speak of the inspiration of Scripture. Here God speaks differently than He does in nature. How are the words of prophets different? Theirs is *special* revelation.

Strictly speaking, we need specific definitions, because technically, even the words *inspiration* and *revelation* are not the same. But though we may use them interchangeably, we are not accurate in doing so. These two terms represent two phases of a prophet's function. *Revelation* represents God's activity as the *composer* and *sender* of a message to His chosen prophet. *Inspiration* represents God's activity upon or within the prophet, helping him to perceive the importance of the message and in becoming the transmitter of that revelation to His people.

God is active in both phases of communicating His message to mankind. He is active in communicating to the prophet; He is active in communicating through the prophet to the people. Beyond the prophetic instrument, God is even active when the prophet's message is read or heard. "Blessed is he that readeth." Revelation 1:3. Although this, of course, does not mean that we as hearers are prophets. God is, in a sense, both Author and Finisher of revelation, from the throne to the believer.

Ellen White, in a simple sentence, makes a helpful *distinction* between revelation and inspiration without attempting a theological definition. She wrote, "I am as dependent upon the Spirit of the Lord in writing my views [inspiration] as I am in receiving them [revelation]."[1]

These two aspects which Mrs. White describes are exactly parallel to what John on Patmos said about his visions. In the opening sentences of the Revelation, John described in detail the steps of God's action in bringing the message from God's throne to you and me. Here again is the description. Count again the steps as you read the verses: "The Revelation of Jesus Christ, which God gave to him, to shew unto his servants the things which must shortly come to pass; and he sent and signified it by his angel unto his servant John." Revelation 1:1. These following steps constitute a working definition of revelation:

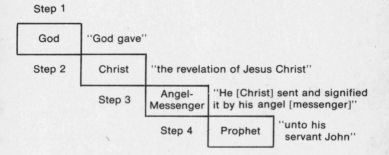

The steps of revelation become even clearer when we add Peter's description, "For the prophecy came not in old time by the will of man: but holy men of God spake as they were moved by the Holy Ghost." 2 Peter 1:21.

Revelation begins with God, is delivered by God the Spirit functioning as the Heavenly Messenger, and received by "holy men [or women]."

The element of inspiration, described in Revelation 1:2, is the last step—step number five: the prophet conveys the message (revelation) to the people. "Who [John] bare record of the word of God, and of the testimony of Jesus Christ, and of all things that he saw. Blessed is he that readeth, and they that hear the words of this prophecy, and keep those things which are written therein." Revelation 1:2, 3.

Here is described the process of writing down or transmitting the message for people to read or hear. Herein the Holy Spirit is active: "Holy men of God spake as they were moved by the Holy Ghost." 2 Peter 1:21. This phenomenon of inspiration is reserved to the prophets whom God Himself selects.

The final result of this process is called in the second verse of Revelation 1 by two names: (1) "the word of God"; (2) "the testimony of Jesus Christ." A synonym for this latter term is mentioned in Revelation 19:10: "For the testimony of Jesus is the spirit of prophecy." While there may be some exceptions and variations, God speaks to you and me through His prophets—by revelation and inspiration.

We think it necessary to emphasize that prophets are chosen by God. "God hath set some in the church, first apostles, secondarily prophets." 1 Corinthians 12:28. In some cases, apostles were also prophets. But no one may study to become a prophet. Being a prophet is a gift of the Spirit, "dividing to every man severally as he will." Verse 11. God chooses prophets to be His spokesmen. That divine calling is included in the meaning of the word *prophet*.

The dependency of a prophet upon the Spirit of the Lord for the message and its transmission is very real. Ellen White referred to this under varied conditions, showing how carefully God superintended the operation of her mind and the accuracy of the message. Note the following illustrations:

The memory loss: "Sometimes the things which I have seen are hid from me after I come out of vision and I cannot call them to mind until I am brought before a company where that vision applies."[2]

The telling and writing: "I am just as dependent upon the Spirit of the Lord in relating or writing a vision, as in having the vision."[3]

The timing: "It is impossible for me to call up things which have been shown me unless the Lord brings

81

them before me at the time that He is pleased to have me relate or write them.''[4]

The control power: "Sometimes even when I am standing before the people, the remembrance comes sharp and clear, like a flash of lightning, bringing to mind distinctly that particular instruction.''[5]

The recall: "Some scenes presented before me years ago have not been retained in my memory, but when the instruction then given is needed . . . the remembrance comes sharp and clear.''[6]

The impelling power: "At such times I cannot refrain from saying the things that flash into my mind, not because I have had a new vision, but because that which was presented to me perhaps years in the past has been recalled to my mind forcibly.''[7]

The letters: "You might say that this communication was only a letter. Yes, it was a letter, but prompted by the Spirit of God, to bring before your minds the things that had been shown me.''[8]

The ideas: "I do not write one article in the paper [Review and Herald] expressing merely my own ideas. They are what God has opened before me in vision.''[9]

These descriptions of inspiration at work are but a tiny sampling of many that might be cited in the E. G. White writings and in Scripture. They are very similar to what the Bible also describes. (Compare Nebuchadnezzar's inability to recall his dream until Daniel presented it anew— Daniel 2:15, 19; Zacharias' loss of speech—Luke 1:22, 64; the control power over Jeremiah—Jeremiah 20:9; John the Baptist's impelling utterance—John 1:29; Isaiah's command to write—Isaiah 30:8; timing control—Ezekiel 3:26; Balaam's restriction on what to speak—Numbers 22:35.

From such experiences one may be assured that

the control factor in inspiration is very strong in a prophet's life. Because of God's involvement revelation and inspiration are reliable, both objectively and subjectively.

Three general theories prevail as to the character of inspiration. Some believe in verbal inspiration, which means that the Holy Spirit controls each word of the prophet. Such see the prophet's writing as that of a secretary taking dictation word for word. Others believe that inspiration is conceptual in character—that the ideas alone are inspired. Third, radical theology of today holds the view of personal inspiration— that inspiration is pure subjectivity and as such renders content unreliable.

According to this theory, prophets are simply persons who are especially perceptive to a far greater degree than ordinary persons are. The inner compulsion to reveal their spiritual insights is so great that it makes them stand out as leaders. Those who hold this view maintain that what was perceived as truth yesterday may be seen as error tomorrow. The Word of God, being primarily a subjective perception of religious themes, is not truth in propositional form. Hence it is not reliable in enunciating eternal principles.

This latter view of inspiration determines one's viewpoint regarding the authority of a prophet's utterances. What results is a Bible that is not theologically authoritative. Those with this viewpoint say that Bible readers may nevertheless be inspired by the words and example of a prophet's great commitment and if so, those words of Scripture should be considered God's word even if the ideas or messages of the prophet were wrong. Thus the authority of the Bible shifts from objective truth to the reader's subjective feeling—a degree of inspiration not subject to objective validation. Seventh-day Adventists reject this theory.

That is why we emphasize that God speaks to the prophets in a way that He does not speak to the rest of us. They became God's spokesmen because they conveyed His messages faithfully. They received the revelation, that is, the content of their messages, by dreams, visions, similitudes, illustrations, and in other ways, but always there was thought content. Under the impress of the Holy Spirit, this thought content was faithfully transmitted by inspiration. That is why prophets could preface their remarks by saying, "The word of the Lord came unto me." In other words, by use of this introduction, the prophets meant, "You can depend on it!" This is the "White truth" regarding the Seventh-day Adventist view of revelation.

It is a dangerous doctrine that substitutes for a divinely given word the reader's subjective feelings. How can a person possibly know whether or not his subjective "inspiration" is good or bad unless he has the objective word of God—the word of all His prophets since the world began—as the norm by which to measure subjective feeling?

Holding such a view of inspiration might be a convenient way to ignore the modern gift of the spirit of prophecy. But doing so would cast us adrift on an open sea of pure subjectivity. Everyone's opinion would then be as valid as anyone else's. One cannot divide the Bible and the spirit of prophecy in this way. There is no such thing as degrees of inspiration with the prophets of God.

What, then, should our position continue to be? Adventists have held that revelation and inspiration have their authority in the validity of thoughts and ideas expressed in the Bible. This is the kind of inspiration Mrs. White described when she wrote these words: "It is not the words of the Bible that are inspired, but the men that were inspired. Inspiration acts not on the man's words or his expressions but on the man himself, who, under the influence of the Holy Ghost, is *imbued with thoughts*. But the words receive the impress of the individual mind. The divine mind is diffused. The divine mind and will is combined with the human mind and will; thus the *utterances of the man are the word of God*."[10]

To recap then, the Seventh-day Adventist Church believes that the Holy Bible is divinely revealed and thus the objective norm for faith and practice. If its authority depended upon the reader's subjective experience to validate its authority, then truth would have no norm. For this reason we reject the personal view of inspiration. We hold to the conceptual view of inspiration because divinely revealed thoughts, ideas, and principles enunciate eternal truth which man can comprehend. As for the verbal view of inspiration, we reject it as a general view, but recognize occasional word-for-word communication from the Lord wherever indicated. Thus we say that revelation to prophets may be a difference in kind but not in degree. This gives us a safe and knowledgeable path in which to walk. It does not set one prophet against another or allow the truths of one age to become error in another. Rather, "the Creator of all ideas may impress different minds with the same thought, but each may express it in a different way, yet without contradiction."[11]

Inspiration stands or falls on the integrity of all its parts. One cannot take out a section from the writings of the Bible prophets or from the writings of Ellen White and say that it is more authoritative than another part or that it is more inspired or less inspired. Such a procedure is not only inconsistent and dangerous, but it also sets up the reader to be the final authority.

To say that Mrs. White did not know the difference between revelation and inspiration does not agree with the facts. The following definition states the phenomenon of revelation about as clearly as it is possible to describe it. "Revelation is not the creation or invention of something new, but the manifestation of that which, until revealed, was unknown to human beings. . . . The Holy Spirit enables the mind to grasp the facts of revelation, and divine light communicates to the soul."[12]

To say that revelation is objective but that inspiration is subjective and hence not reliable makes the testimonies of a prophet suspect and thus unreliable. This is merely another device to make of no effect the authority of God's prophets. "Believe his prophets, so shall ye prosper." 2 Chronicles 20:20.

Many years ago a series of articles were written in the *Review and Herald* advocating degrees of inspiration in the Bible. The articles tended to show that some parts were inspired, some were not—that some were authority and some were not. It brought a just rebuke from Ellen White: "Both in the [Battle Creek] Tabernacle and in the college the subject of inspiration has been taught, and finite men have taken it upon themselves to say that some things in the Scriptures were inspired and some were not. I was shown that the Lord did not inspire the articles on inspiration published in the *Review*, neither did He approve their endorsement before our youth in the college. When men venture to criticize the Word of God, they venture on sacred, holy ground, and had better fear and tremble and hide their wisdom as foolishness."[13]

Divine messages may not be categorized by degrees

of inspiration. They stand or fall together. Of her own writings, Ellen White made a similar observation: "There is no half-way work in the matter. The *Testimonies* are of the Spirit of God, or of the devil."[14]

There are ways to test the validity of a claim to inspiration: The content of the revelation must be in harmony with the Bible. The life and work of the prophet must be above reproach. The prophetic manifestation must answer to the biblical doctrine of the gift of prophecy and fulfill the predictions of its witness in the life of the remnant in our day.

We believe Ellen White meets these tests in every detail. One of the refreshing benefits in reading about Mrs. White's life and work is to see the principles of revelation and inspiration at work in her everyday living. (This emerges constantly in the manuscript for the six-volume biography of Ellen G. White, the first volume of which is now available.) This is far more impressive than reading mere theological theory about these principles. The experience of the Salamanca vision is a practical example of this, which not only instructs but inspires.

On one of Mrs. White's speaking itineraries in 1890, she stayed overnight in the Hicks home in Salamanca, New York. That night she experienced a vision. The next morning she began to tell it to her son, W. C. White, and to A. T. Robinson: "I want to tell you about what was revealed to me last night. For in the vision I seemed to be in Battle Creek, and the angel messenger bade me, 'Follow me.' "

Suddenly she hesitated. She could remember no more. The two men visited awhile and were about to leave, when she tried again: "I want to tell you about what was revealed to me last night. It had to do with important matters. In the vision I seemed to be in Battle Creek, and I was taken to the Review and Herald building, and the angel messenger bade me, 'Follow me—.'"

Again she could remember no more.

Her journal records that the vision concerned the policies of the *American Sentinel*—the religious-liberty journal of that day. A few sentences give the gist of what she saw: "I heard words repeated by influential men to the effect that if the *American Sentinel* would drop the words 'Seventh-day Adventist' from its columns, and would say nothing about the Sabbath, the great men of the world would patronize it."

About four months after this vision the General Conference was held in Battle Creek. Mrs. White spoke at 5:30 each morning and on Sabbath afternoon. At the Sabbath afternoon meeting she attempted to share the contents of her vision with the congregation. She began to speak: "I must tell you of the vision which was given me at Salamanca; for in that vision important matters were revealed to me. In the vision I seemed to be in Battle Creek. I was taken to the *Review and Herald* office, and the angel messenger bade me, 'Follow me.'"

She hesitated. Later in her sermon she began again, faltered, and went on. The recollection had gone from her. A third time she began but was unable to tell it. Finally, she said, "Of this I shall have more to say later"; and she closed her sermon without telling it. All had noticed the problem and wondered about it.

Elder Olsen, the General Conference president, asked if she would speak again the next morning; but she declined, saying that she had spoken, was tired, and would rest.

That night a small group of men met in the Review office to discuss the editorial policy of the *American*

Sentinel. Someone locked the door, proposing that they stay until the problem was settled. They remained there till 3:00 a.m., deadlocked. Finally the meeting closed with one man voicing a threat that unless they removed the terms *Seventh-day Adventist* and *Sabbath* from the magazine's columns they would no longer use the paper as the organ of the Religious Liberty Association.

Shortly after 3:00 a.m., Mrs. White was awakened and instructed that she must present the Salamanca vision at the 5:30 meeting.

Elder White, her son, was keenly interested. Five times he had heard her begin to relate the vision, only to find herself unable to finish. At the morning meeting, Elder Olsen was surprised to see her and asked if she had a message.

"Indeed I do," she replied. Stepping to the front, she said, "I was aroused at 3:00 a.m. this morning and instructed to bear a testimony as to a vision I was shown in Salamanca."

"In the vision," she went on, "I seemed to be in Battle Creek. I was taken to the Review and Herald office, and the angel messenger bade me, 'Follow me.' I was taken to a room where a group of men were earnestly discussing a matter." After further describing the meeting, she continued. "I saw one of the men take a copy of the *Sentinel*, hold it high over his head, and say, 'Unless these articles on Sabbath and the second advent come out of this paper, we can no longer use it as the organ of the Religious Liberty Association.'"

She spoke for an hour, giving her counsel. One man followed another, to speak in response. One said, "I was in that meeting last night." Mrs. White remarked in surprise, "Last night! I thought it happened months ago when it was shown me in vision." The man speaking continued, "I was in that meeting last night, and I am the man who made the remarks about the articles in the paper, holding it high over my head. I am sorry to say that I was on the wrong side; but I take this opportunity to place myself on the right side." Others testified as to the accuracy of her description and confessed their errors in spirit and judgment.[15]

Why was it that five times before, she was not allowed to share that vision? If she had told it or had written it out and sent it, it would have been denied because it had not yet taken place. Or the meeting would not have been held.

This incident, like others in her ministry, bears witness to the nature of inspiration and shows that prophets of God speak as they are "moved by the Holy Ghost." Such experiences give us confidence to believe in the authority of the prophet's words. Yes, revelation is authentic. And inspiration, too, is thoroughly dependable. You can count on it.

The Truth About Lies

A lie is not the truth; the truth is not a lie. A lie always parades as truth; the truth never parades as a lie. A lie will call the truth a lie; the truth never calls a lie the truth.

We also should draw a distinction between an honest mistake and a lie. A mistake becomes a lie only when an attempt to deceive is present. For example, one may for years set forth a point that eventually is proven contrary to fact. But if the writer (or speaker) was himself misinformed and had no intent to deceive, he did not lie. He merely inadvertently passed on mistaken information—an honest mistake.

Casting aspersion upon the truth or even an honest mistake is a favorite device of a lie. Should such charges be dignified with an answer? Is it better to let the dust settle—or to keep it stirred by the winds of debate? Or should we simply state the truth—and leave it there.

The truth is that Ellen G. White and the church have been accused of dealing in "white lies." Whether the epithet is spelled with an initial capital letter or in lowercase, the charge is not a matter of slight importance. The term *lie* simply does not square with the known record of Mrs. White's ministry and message.

Her contributions to the church are substantial, uplifting, and positive. We would like to illuminate the white lie charge with the truth.

The truth about the "White" lie accusations is that Mrs. White is either a prophet of the Lord or she is not. You can't have her as a nice, little, well-meaning lady—but! She surely shouldn't be given a place of honor as one of the founders of the Adventist Church if she is a fraud. The church, too, so reflects the guidance of the spirit of prophecy that it cannot disassociate itself from the gift. If she is a fraud, the church is a fraud. Mrs. White herself met this issue directly.

"This work is of God, or it is not. God does nothing in partnership with Satan. My work . . . bears the stamp of God or the stamp of the enemy. There is no halfway work in the matter. The *Testimonies* are of the Spirit of God, or of the devil."[1]

What is the evidence? The whole of her work and its results! Her response to the question is positive. In reply to such charges she wrote—not so much in defense as in appeal: "As the Lord has manifested Himself through the spirit of prophecy, past, present and future have passed before me. I have been shown faces that I have never seen, and years afterward I knew them when I saw them. I have been aroused from my sleep with a vivid sense of subjects previously presented to my mind; and I have written, at midnight, letters that have gone across the continent and, arriving at a crisis, have saved great disaster to the cause of God. This has been my work for many years. A power has impelled me to reprove and rebuke wrongs that I had not thought of. Is this work of the last thirty-six years [eventually seventy] from above or from beneath?"[2]

That question must be individually answered. One

must take a sober look at the whole sweep of her dynamic contributions, make a considered judgment, and take a stand.

A recent letter to the editor of *Ministry*, apparently written by a minister, speaks of a similar decision he had been forced to make about a pair of verses in the Scriptures. One was Numbers 25:9, which states that 24,000 people died in a plague. However, when he compared this to 1 Corinthians 10:8, he found that Paul said 23,000 died in that plague. Here was his reaction to the discrepancy: "For some reason this greatly disturbed me, and I sat flipping my Bible back and forth from one passage to the other, unable to believe my eyes, since I do believe in the inerrancy of the Bible. After quite some time of earnest prayer, asking the Lord, 'What does this mean?' He answered, 'It means that you are a lot more nit-picky about details than I am.'"[3]

Quite possibly what may seem to be a "white lie" is not one at all but simply appears to be so because of one's own faulty opinion of how inspiration and revelation ought to operate. He who focuses upon the fallible human instrument misses the power behind the instrument. Mrs. White was quite aware of the difference. "In regard to infallibility, I never claimed it; God alone is infallible."[4]

The central question is not, however, some picky detail. The central question to settle is whether or not Mrs. White was a prophet of the Lord. No confusion or doubt about this lingered in the mind of Ellen White as reflected in her own statements about her work. She knew the difference between divine revelation and mere subjective reflection and understood her role as coming down squarely on the side of revelation. Her statement is to the point: "The Lord has manifested Himself through the spirit of prophecy." That's clear. "Past, present and future have passed before me." That's definite. "I have been shown faces." That's solid. If all this is from above, she is a prophet.

God never forces the intellect so as to bypass our freedom to choose. In the very nature of the divine-human exchange, room remains for questions. Yet God always provides sufficient evidence for the honest seeker to believe that He has sent His "messenger" as He has promised in His Word to do.

In this small book, our purpose has been to address the principles related to the larger premise rather than to engage in a debate over details. By grasping positive principles, the student will have the tools to deal with any doubts raised about the Lord's guidance in our past history.

Most of the allegations charging that Mrs. White's reputation is dependent upon lies are aimed at her originality, authority, or integrity. We have already dealt with these areas in previous chapters. But in these last few pages we'll consider a few specifics.

Originality. We have heard a lot about Mrs. White's literary borrowings, in an apparent effort to discredit her originality. The chapters on plagiarism and sources have touched on that. But more may be said about the truth of Ellen White's originality.

The truth is that the uniqueness of Mrs. White's messages was dependent upon her many visions. Recently it was my privilege to be permitted two weeks of unrestricted access to the documents in the Ellen White vault in Washington, D.C. I read all the manuscripts and letters covering a four-year stretch in the mid-1880s. Letter after letter contained such authenticating words as "My instructor said," "I saw," "Your case passed before me," or equivalent phrases. Most manuscripts were similarly sprinkled with these reassuring phrases.

These "I saws" were not restricted to the early days of her ministry but seemed to be a general practice. The margins of the letters and manuscripts often indicated the release of a particular paragraph for publication in one book or another. And while the released portions themselves may not have contained the familiar authenticating phrase indicating a revelation, such a validating phrase was nearly always somewhere in the letter from which they were taken.

I came away convinced that there must be hundreds of such authenticating phrases. I had heard mentioned the figure of 2000 visions, and I asked Arthur L. White, long-time secretary of the White Estate, for the source of that estimate. He replied, "I suppose I am responsible for it. While I have not made an actual count, yet from my many years of handling the documents and reading them, that figure appeared to me as a conservative and reasonable estimate." I, too, came away feeling that there was no reason to doubt the estimate of 2000 visions.

That would amount to about one vision every two weeks for seventy years and Arthur White declared that, often, they were more frequent than that. Little wonder that Mrs. White spent so much of her time with a pen in her hand. What a constant and living connection with Heaven must have been hers! Just a few days of reading documents assured me that whatever their number, there had obviously been many, many visions!

As I thoughtfully read some of her own handwriting, I remembered these words, "After I come out of vision I do not at once remember all that I have seen, and the matter is not so clear before me until I write, then the scene rises before me as presented in vision, and I can write it with freedom.''[5]

With the realization that in my hand was the evidence that inspiration had been at work while those words were being penned decades ago, a solemnity—quite inexplicable—passed over me. I could picture the pen tracing out those words which she wrote as moved by the Holy Ghost. Though Ellen White died before I was born, yet her messages are as fresh and as clear as today's sunshine.

For me, it was a precious experience to realize that, while no original manuscripts of the Bible prophets exist anywhere, yet in my hands were the original documents of how the Lord has spoken in our day. Yet it was even more solemnizing to note that the final step in the revelatory process takes place when the Holy Spirit makes those ideas live in the reader who ''listens.'' You may remember Ellen White's words: ''Whether or not my life is spared, my writing shall constantly speak, and their work will go forward as long as time shall last.''[6] The important question for me is this: Is the dear Saviour using them to speak to me? He will if I read with an open heart. I have found it so.

The truth is that originality is discovered time after time by those who prayerfully read the Ellen White books. The church has recognized it too. It cannot be proved, though, any more than Scripture can be proved. One person says that the Bible prophets were fakes. Another says that their words are the very word of God. Each reader for himself must discover the truth of originality. I have made the discovery and affirm it. I have found an original quality in Mrs. White's writings that speaks as other books, aside from the Scriptures, do not. I am not alone in that discovery.

That is what Attorney Vincent L. Ramik, a senior partner in a Washington, D.C., legal firm specializing in copyright law, discovered. He began a critical examination of her books with a bias that she was a plagiarist, but something unexpected happened. Though he was looking for literary theft, after 300 hours studying the charges against her, he said there simply was no case.[7] Besides the strictly legal facts of the case, something else impressed him to turn 180 degrees in his attitude.

"Now there are a lot of things that Mrs. White has put down on paper that will, if read seriously, perhaps cause a person to look inwardly, honestly. And if you do, the true self comes out; I think I know a little more about the real Vince Ramik than I did before I started reading the *message* of Ellen White, not simply her *writings*. . . . Quite honestly, I think I've left this task with more than I've put into it. And it's simply her messages. . . . It makes you believe a little more firmly in things you may have believed a little bit less in the past.

"Mrs. White moved me! In all candor, she moved me. I am a Roman Catholic; but Catholic, Protestant whatever—she moved me. And I think her writings should move anyone, unless he is permanently biased and is unswayable."[8]

Thousands can testify to the truth of that statement. In her writings is a power and originality which the church recognizes as the prophetic voice. Her messages reveal credentials of a kind many find nowhere else outside of the Scriptures. The writings are authoritative because of their origin. Ellen White recognized that she was not the originator of her books and

97

did not take credit to herself. "Of myself I could not have brought out the truth in these books, but the Lord has given me the help of His Holy Spirit."[9] Those visions, those scenes that passed before her, and the accompanying explanations provided her, give to her writing the freshness of an eyewitness and the richness of an authentic firsthand report.

Messages such as these have not been duplicated in any contemporary writer, it seems to me. This fact becomes all the more apparent when one compares even some of her earliest little books like *Christian Experience and Views* or *Spiritual Gifts* which now comprise *Early Writings*. The same stark, literary simplicity and directness shines through these earlier books as in her later, more expanded works. Even when she employed the beautiful and descriptive language of others, a certain something happened to those jewels as she reset them for her own purposes. In being recast to fit her message, they shone with more power, appeal, and beauty than the sources from which they were taken. This intangible and singular quality is evident in all of her books and is often recognized by those who come upon them for the first time.

Her use of the descriptions and phraseology of others in presenting her messages needs to be seen through nineteenth-century glasses. George H. Callcott, in his recent *History in the United States, 1800-1860*, published by The John Hopkins Press in 1970, speaks about the custom of historians of those years in "using as their own works the same phraseology as someone else had used."[10] If anyone had raised the cry of plagiarism, the accused historian "would have been dismayed by the attack . . . and would simply have pointed out that he had never intended to be original when he could find someone else who had satisfactorily said what he had in mind."[11] Again, "Historians usually felt flattered rather than insulted when their words were used by another."[12]

"The period is remarkable for the lack of scholarly rivalry, and writers who borrowed from each other remained on the warmest of terms."[13] The author adds that this kind of relationship was not a rare one but was the typical point of view of nineteenth-century historians. Modern scholars have attacked historians of the period such as William Gordon and John Marshall. Gordon used material from the *Annual Register* without quotation marks; but Gordon was not dishonest, because in his introduction he carefully explained that he had "frequently quoted from them without varying the language, except for method and conciseness."[14] Callcott adds that this was done with "pride rather than apology" and says Gordon explained further that he had "at times inserted them as though they were originally my own."[15] John Marshall similarly explained his use of sources, saying, "The very language has sometimes been employed without distinguishing the passages . . . by marks of quotation."[16] How similar that compares with Mrs. White's Introduction to *The Great Controversy*.

To judge the past by present custom is often tempting. But not necessarily scholarly. Callcott, in 1970, further observes that "the early nineteenth-century historian felt no need to argue for originality, and he would not have understood why he should make a fetish of reworking material when what he wanted to say already had been said better by another. . . . It appeared entirely proper to borrow literally as well as factually. The unfolding of the story was more important than the fear that the author would receive undeserved credit for eloquence."[17] They simply used the writings of another as a vehicle for what they wanted to say. Ellen White's claim to originality was not in the phraseology she employed but in her treatment of the content in harmony with what God had originally shown her.

Mrs. White maintained the same relationship to other authors and publishers as Callcott describes her contemporaries as holding. In fact, correspondence from the publisher of Conybeare and Howson's *Life and Epistles of the Apostle Paul* suggests just such a relationship. In 1924, C. E. Holmes, an employee of the Review and Herald Publishing Association, directed the following inquiry to the Crowell Company in New York: "Some years ago you published a book entitled 'Life and Epistles of the Apostle Paul.' In 1883 a book was printed by the Review and Herald Publishing Co., of Battle Creek, Mich., entitled 'Sketches From the Life of Paul.' For a long time it has been claimed that because of a similarity of ideas and words in several instances in this book, you at one time threatened prosecution unless the book was withdrawn from circulation.

"This report is now being scattered about in printed form and I should be pleased to know if there is any truth in it. Any information that you can give regarding this matter will be greatly appreciated."

Three days later, Mr. T. Y. Crowell replied,

"Your letter of Jan. 15th received. We publish Conybeare's *Life and Epistles of the Apostle Paul* but this is not a copyrighted book and we would have no legal grounds for action against your book and we do not think we have ever raised any objection or made any claim such as you speak of."[18]

The question was raised back in 1924. It need not have been raised then. It need not be raised now. It shouldn't come up in the future. But don't count on it.

Even the troubled Fannie Bolton, four years after being dropped from her role as a literary assistant by Ellen White for the third and final time, volunteered the following confession: "I rebelled in heart against what I considered the taking of undue credit on the part of Sister White in receiving unqualified commendations for books or articles upon which Marian Davis, myself and others had expended editorial work."[19]

From this it would seem that her real problem was just as she stated it, rather than any concern about whether Ellen White cited her sources properly. No such desire for recognition ever troubled Marian Davis, whose work was even more extensive in nature than Bolton's. Fannie Bolton was not incorrect, either, in making these observations: "prophetic inspiration is vastly above the editor's knowledge of the words of any human author, and vastly above what Sister White could possibly bring forth herself. . . . God is the author of all truth, and has a right to choose what He shall make use of in the work of His Spirit."[20]

"I thank God that He has kept Sister White from following my supposed superior wisdom and righteousness, and has kept her from acknowledging editors and authors. . . . Had she done as I wished her to do, the gift would have been degraded to a common authorship, its importance lost, its authority undermined and its blessings lost to the world."[21]

Authority. The truth is that the authority of Mrs. White as a prophet is witnessed in the fruitage of her word and ministry. Although the church recognizes it in its official statements of faith, this recognition does not bestow its authority. Neither can the critics of that authority take it away. It is not a man-made myth—it is a reality.

Often it has been observed that one can throw more dust in the air in a second than another can settle in an hour. To make demeaning accusations does not make them true. To say that it is but legend that Adventist pioneers believed that Mrs. White spoke with the prophetic authority of the spirit of prophecy is not in accord with the many official resolutions of the early General Conference in session or with the written works of the pioneers. To allege that the church, in holding to the Bible as its only rule of faith and practice, must therefore relinquish the authority accorded the writings of Ellen White does not make it so. Opposers cannot avoid the simple fact that the Bible, within itself, contains the evidence that prophets are subject to the prophets. To proclaim that Mrs. White, however well intentioned, did not know the difference between revelation and inspiration is contrary to the body of material she wrote in explaining the subject. To dust off and play again the scratchy old records of earlier Ellen White critics does not make them more credible on the replay.

The real truth about the spirit of prophecy is above such detractions. The view that the Bible and the Bible alone is the rule of faith and practice does not destroy the authority of the gift of prophecy. To allow this would be to disallow those very portions of the Bible that promise the gift of prophecy as God should choose to give it until the end of time. Bible prophets coming upon the scene through the centuries did not demean themselves by deferring to the prophets who had gone before. The selection by the church of the prophetic books ultimately included in the Bible provides a good illustration of how the authority of prophets is not diminished by the rule that all prophets must be subject to the prophets who have spoken before.

If it be true that through prophets of past ages the Lord has communicated doctrine, what logic would deny Him the right to clarify those doctrines through a prophet today or to confirm as truth or error any human doctrine that claims to be hewn from the Word? Ellen White's stated purpose was not to bring in some new doctrine but to confirm those already revealed in Scripture. Certainly, when one sees hundreds of denominations reaching contradictory conclusions—all supposedly basing their teachings on the same Scriptures—the need and value of a revelation through the testimony of Jesus should be apparent.

The fact that Ellen White, at times, utilized the expressions of other authors in accomplishing her task—in presenting the Lord's message for these last times—is really inconsequential. It has very little to do with the central issue. Neither will it matter if researchers ever discover exactly how much or how little she was assisted in her presentation of truth by the wording in books written by others. What *does* matter is whether or not she was God's "messenger."

Finally, the truth about the authority of Mrs. White will not be decided by repeating hackneyed objections. There have always been those who overlook the monumental stones of accomplishment because they stumble over such supposed pebbles as "the shut door," "food for worms," or a six o'clock Sabbath, and other such warmed-over objections. Were as much effort spent on seeking answers to honest questions as in raising doubts anew, we might be about our Father's business.

"The shut door!" Really! That again? Ellen White's explanation still sounds better than the objection. "With my brethren and sisters, after the time passed in forty-four I did believe no more sinners

would be converted. But I never had a vision that no more sinners would be converted. . . . It was on my first journey east [1845] to relate my visions that the precious light in regard to the heavenly sanctuary was opened before me and I was shown the open and shut door. . . . I was shown that there was a great work to be done in the world for those who had not had the light and rejected it. . . . Those who rejected the light which was brought into the world by the message of the second angel went into darkness."[22]

Although her understanding of the open and shut door broadened and was further clarified in the five years following 1844, it was always consistent with her first vision on the subject, which included the closing of the door of the first apartment (of the sanctuary) and the opening of the second. Books have been written on this, but why should it take up further space?

"Food for worms." This phrase is taken from the following statement: "I was shown the company present at the Conference. Said the angel, 'Some food for worms, some subjects of the seven last plagues, some will be alive and remain upon the earth to be translated at the coming of Jesus.'"[23]

What shall we say about this? Obviously, the people living in 1858 have passed off the scene of action. Does that make Mrs. White a false prophet? Jonah preached, "Yet forty days, and Nineveh shall be overthrown." Was Jonah therefore a false prophet? The principle Jonah was addressing was real: Sin brings judgment. Because of Nineveh's response to Jonah's message the judgment promised Nineveh was postponed. Yet there had been no "if" in Jonah's proclamation. The delayed judgment perplexed and angered the prophet. But conditions again changed and Nineveh's sins brought judgment and destruction 150 years later. Still, not one to whom Jonah preached ever saw the fulfillment.

Jonah was not a false prophet, nor was Ellen White. Jonah was wrong, however, to question the delay occasioned by God's mercy. Ellen White's explanation regarding the delay of the advent reported in such places as *Selected Messages*, book 1, pages 67-69, is in harmony with biblical principles regarding how God will conclude the great controversy between good and evil.

"A six o'clock Sabbath." Why did not Mrs. White from the very first correct the error of a 6:00 sunset time as the beginning of the Sabbath? Let James White answer the question. "It does not appear to be the desire of the Lord to teach his people by the gifts of the Spirit on the Bible questions until his servants have diligently searched his Word. When this was done upon the subject of time to commence the Sabbath, and most were established, and some were in danger of being out of harmony with the body on this subject, then, yes, *then*, was the very time for God to magnify his goodness in the manifestation of the gift of his Spirit."[24]

Here he was referring to the 1855 conference, where the subject of the time to commence the Sabbath was discussed and a paper by J. N. Andrews was read in favor of the "even to even" concept. At the close of the conference Ellen White received a vision. James White reported, "Mrs. W. had a vision, one item of which was that the sunset time was correct. This settled the matter with Bro. Bates and others, and general harmony has since prevailed among us upon this point."[25]

Items like these serve to illustrate the frivolous character of some of the stock objections that have repeatedly surfaced since early days. From time to time someone who has reservations or is hostile will dust them off as new discoveries. What is indeed a mystery is the *uncritical acceptance* by some of all that seems to detract from her life and work and the *uncritical rejection* of that which is favorable and supported by abundant evidence.

Integrity. Integrity is a strong word. To accuse Mrs. White and the church of not measuring up, of lacking integrity, is tantamount to full rejection of her as a prophet and repudiation of the church which supports her. How could there be any moral soundness, simple honesty, and uprightness without integrity? How could she be a Christian—let alone a prophet— without it? A person is either honest or dishonest. A person cannot be a little dishonest and still be honest. Not even a white lie will do.

The truth, happily, is that we can say she was demonstrably honest in her use of sources. What would be sad would be proof to the contrary. But there is no such proof. The facts indicate her conduct to be both morally and legally blameless. She hides nothing. She recommends that people read the books she has used. She breaks no copyright laws. She explains in print how she used the writings of others and her purposes in doing so. She is in full compliance with the prevailing conventions of her time. She comes through with flying colors.

One seeming discrepancy or another is often seized upon to cast doubt upon her integrity. Some have insinuated that she prevaricated when she said, "I did not read any books upon health until I had written Spiritual Gifts, Vols. iii and iv, Appeal to Mothers, and had sketched out most of my six articles in the six numbers of 'How to Live.' "[26] Her comprehensive health vision occurred on June 6, 1863. *Appeal to Mothers* was printed in April 1864, *Spiritual Gifts* in August 1864.

Later on, Mrs. White read the purchased books and used them. "After I had written my six articles for 'How to Live', I then searched the various works on hygiene and was surprised to find them so nearly in harmony with what the Lord has revealed to me. And to show this harmony, and to set before my brethren and sisters the subject as brought out by able writers, I determined to publish 'How to Live,' in which I largely extracted from the works referred to."[27]

By this she meant that these selections from other writers (such as L. B. Coles) on similar subjects were printed along with her own six articles for the sake of comparison. They appeared in articles under the by-lines of their authors in the very same pamphlets. In later years she incorporated some of their language into some of her own writings. Critics found these later writings and thought they had discovered a covert theft on her part. As you would expect, Mrs. White's integrity is unimpeachable.

People will believe what they want to believe. That cannot be stopped. Nor is it our task to judge the motives of anyone. Still, it is always a mystery as to how some can suddenly jettison that which they have held dear for years as truth, call it error, then fight aginst it bitterly. This happened in heaven (Revelation 12)—and has happened often since. It makes one tremble and pray, "lead us not into temptation, but deliver us from evil," for "It is not in man to direct his steps."

Two unsophisticated men were sightseeing abroad. When in Paris they decided to visit the Louvre. As they viewed the famed art treasures, they were not impressed with the value of the priceless oil paintings. Standing before an especially noted masterpiece, one said to the other, "Imagine that being worth a million dollars! I don't see what's so special about it. You'd certainly never catch me paying a fortune for it." The guard, overhearing the conversation, quietly stepped up to the man, touched him on the elbow, and said, "I couldn't help but overhear your conversation. I would like to say, Sir, that these paintings are not on trial, but those who come to see them are!"

So it is with God's prophets. Daniel was not on trial in the lions' den. Babylon was. Jeremiah was not on trial in the pit. Zedekiah was. Paul, standing with chains before Agrippa, was not on trial. The king was. And Jesus, that greatest of prophets and King of kings, standing accused before the Praetorium, was not on trial. Pilate and His accusers were.

Jehoshaphat's appeal to his people was, "Hear me, O Judah, and ye inhabitants of Jerusalem; Believe in the Lord your God, so shall ye be established; believe his prophets, so shall ye prosper." 2 Chronicles 20:20.

Ellen White's appeal to the movement dearest to her heart was this: "In reviewing our past history, having traveled over every step of advance to our present standing, I can say, Praise God! As I see what the Lord has wrought, I am filled with astonishment, and with confidence in Christ as leader. We have nothing to fear for the future, except as we shall forget the way the Lord has led us, and His teaching in our past history."[28]

My appeal is, Remember that Mrs. White is not on trial. Those of us who read her are.

REFERENCES

The Truth About Sources

1. John Dart, "Plagiarism Found in Prophet Books," *Los Angeles Times*, October 21, 1980.

2. Uriah Smith, *The Visions of Mrs. E. G. White, a Manifestation of Spiritual Gifts According to the Scriptures* (Battle Creek, Mich.: Battle Creek Steam Press, 1868).

3. F. M. Wilcox, *The Testimony of Jesus* (Washington, D.C.: Review and Herald Publishing Association, 1934) p. 112.

4. Ellen G. White, *The Great Controversy* (Mountain View, Calif.: Pacific Press Publishing Association, 1911) p. x. (The paging of the author's Introduction as found in certain printings exceeds those noted here by two pages. Page x in some printings is page xii in others, etc.)

5. *Ibid.*, pp. xi, xii.

6. Ellen G. White, Letter 56, 1911.

7. Ellen G. White, *Colporteur Ministry* (Mountain View, Calif.: Pacific Press Publishing Association, 1953) p. 125.

8. Ellen G. White, *Testimonies for the Church* (Mountain View, Calif.: Pacific Press Publishing Association, 1948), vol. 5, p. 67.

9. Ellen G. White, *The Great Controversy,* pp. xi, xii.

10. *Ibid.*, p. xi.

The Truth About Plagiarism

1. Ellen G. White, *The Great Controversy*, p. xii.

2. See *Adventist Review*, Sept. 17, 1981, pp. 3-7.

3. William Allan Edwards, *Plagiarism: An Essay on Good and Bad Borrowing* (Cambridge, England: Gordon Fraser, The Minority Press, 1933), pp. 6, 114 (emphasis supplied).

4. John Harris, *The Great Teacher*, second edition, (Amherst: J.S. & C. Adams, 1836) pp. 33, 34.

5. Interview with Hon. Robert D. Macomber, Riverside, Calif., Sept. 1981.

6. *Review and Herald*, Jan. 9, 1883.

7. *Signs of the Times*, Jan. 18, 1883.

8. *Review and Herald*, Dec. 26, 1882.

9. Ellen G. White, *The Great Controversy*, p. xii.

10. W. C. White and Dores Robinson, *Brief Statements* (St. Helena, Calif.: Elmshaven office, Aug. 1933), p. 5. Reprinted as a supplement in *Adventist Review*, June 4, 1981.

11. The thoughts and some of the words expressed here are similar to those of John Harris in his book *The Great Teacher*, pp. 35, 89 and 91.

12. Ellen G. White, Manuscript 25, 1890.

13. *Ibid.*

14. Ellen G. White, *Testimonies*, vol. 5, p. 67.

The Truth About Prophets

1. *Church Manual*, (Washington, D.C.: General Conference of Seventh-day Adventists, 1971), p. 37.

2. *Seventh-day Adventist Yearbook*, 1981 (Washington, D.C.: Review and Herald Publishing Association), p. 7.

3. Ellen G. White, *Testimonies*, vol. 8, p. 91.

4. "A Statement Refuting Charges Made by A. T. Jones Against the Spirit of Prophecy and the Plan of Organization of the Seventh-day Adventist Denomination" (Washington, D.C.: General Conference Committee, 1906) p. 81.

5. *Ibid.*, p. 85.

6. *Ibid.*, p. 83.

7. Ellen G. White, *Review and Herald*, Jan. 26, 1905.

8. Ellen G. White, *Selected Messages* (Washington, D.C.: Review and Herald Publishing Association, 1980), bk. 1, pp. 35, 36.

9. *Ibid.*, p. 34.

10. Ibid., p. 36

11. Ellen G. White, Selected Messages, bk. 1, p. 36.

12. Ellen G. White, *Colporteur Ministry*, p. 125.

13. Ellen G. White, *The Great Controversy*, p. vii.

The Truth About Authority

1. Ellen G. White, *Selected Messages*, bk. 1, p. 55.

2. Ellen G. White, *Life Sketches of Ellen G. White* (Mountain View, Calif.: Pacific Press Publishing Association, 1915) p. 196 (emphasis supplied).

3. Don F. Neufeld, ed., *Seventh-day Adventist Encyclopedia*, rev. ed. (Washington, D.C.: Review and Herald Publishing Association, 1976), p. 762.

4. Ellen G. White, *Counsels to Writers and Editors* (Nashville, Tenn.: Southern Publishing Association) p. 30.

5. Ellen G. White, *Selected Messages*, bk. 3, pp. 31, 32.

6. *Ibid.*, p. 32 (emphasis supplied).

7. *Ibid.*

8. Ellen G. White, *Testimonies*, vol. 9, p. 69. See also Ellen G.

White, *Gospel Workers* (Washington, D.C.: Review and Herald Publishing Association, 1920), p. 307.

9. Ellen G. White, *Selected Messages*, bk. 3, p. 32.

10. *Ibid.*, pp. 32, 33.

11. *Ibid.*

12. Ellen G. White, *Testimonies*, vol. 5, p. 676.

13. Ellen G. White, *Counsels to Writers and Editors*, pp. 31, 32.

14. Ellen G. White, Manuscript 59, 1905.

15. Ellen G. White, Manuscript 44, 1905.

16. Ellen G. White, Manuscript 125, 1907

17. Ellen G. White, Letter 208, 1906. Letter to Elder Tenney.

18. Ellen G. White, Letter 329, 1905. Letter to Elder Burden.

19. Ellen G. White, Letter 50, 1906. Letter to Elder Simpson.

20. Ellen G. White, *The Great Controversy*, p. 595.

21. Ellen G. White, *Selected Messages, bk. 3, p. 32.*

22. *Ibid.*

23. James White, "Time to Commence the Sabbath," *Review and Herald*, Feb. 25, 1868.

24. J. N. Loughborough, "Recollections of the Past," *Review and Herald*, March 3, 1885, p. 138.

25. J. N. Andrews, "Our Use of the Visions of Sr. White," *Review and Herald*, Feb. 15, 1879, p. 39 (emphasis supplied).

26. G. I. Butler, "The Visions," *Review and Herald*, Aug. 14, 1883.

27. Ellen G. White, *Selected Messages*, bk. 1, p. 37.

28. F. M. Wilcox, "The Testimony of Jesus," *Review and Herald*, June 9, 1946, p. 61.

29. *Selected Messages*, bk. 1, p. 57.

The Truth About Inspiration and Revelation

1. Ellen G. White, "Questions and Answers," *Review and Herald*, Oct. 8, 1867.

2. Ellen G. White, *Selected Messages*, bk. 1, p. 36.

3. *Ibid.*

4. *Ibid.*, pp. 36, 37.

5. *Ibid.*, p. 37.

6. *Ibid.*

7. *Ibid.*

8. Ellen G. White, *Testimonies*, vol. 5, p. 67.

9. Ellen G. White, *Selected Messages*, bk. 1, p. 27.

10. *Ibid.*, p. 21 (emphasis supplied).

11. *Ibid.*, p. 22.

12. Ellen G. White, Manuscript 59, 1906.

13. Ellen G. White, *Selected Messages*, bk. 1, p. 23.

14. Ellen G. White, *Testimonies*, vol. 4, p. 230.

15. T. H. Jemison, *A Prophet Among You* (Mountain View, Calif.: Pacific Press Publishing Association, 1955) pp. 471-480.

The Truth About Lies

1. Ellen G. White, *Testimonies*, vol. 4, p. 230.
2. *Ibid.*, vol. 5, p. 671.
3. "Letters," *Ministry*, Sept. 1981, p. 2.
4. Ellen G. White, *Selected Messages*, bk. 1, p. 37.
5. *Ibid.*, p. 36.
6. *Ibid.*, p. 55.
7. See *Adventist Review*, Sept. 17, 1981, pp. 3-7.
8. *Ibid.*, p. 4.
9. Ellen G. White, *Selected Messages*, bk. 1, p. 35.
10. George G. Callcott, *History In the United States, 1800-1860* (Baltimore, Md.: The Johns Hopkins Press, 1970) p. 134.
11. *Ibid.*
12. *Ibid.*, p. 136.
13. *Ibid.*
14. *Ibid.*, p. 135.
15. *Ibid.*
16. *Ibid.*
17. *Ibid.*
18. Quoted in Francis D. Nichol, *Ellen White and Her Critics* (Washington, D.C.: Review and Herald Publishing Association, 1951) pp. 455-457.
19. Fannie Bolton, "A Confession Concerning the Testimony of Jesus Christ" (Washington, D.C.: Ellen G. White Estate, document D.F. 445), p. 3.
20. *Ibid.*, pp. 5, 6.
21. *Ibid.*, p. 8.
22. Ellen G. White, *Selected Messages*, bk. 1, p. 74.
23. Ellen G. White, *Testimonies*, vol. 1, pp. 131, 132.
24. Quoted in Francis D. Nichol, *Ellen White and Her Critics*, p. 354.
25. *Ibid.*, p. 353.
26. "Questions and Answers," *Review and Herald*, October 8, 1867.
27. *Ibid.*
28. Ellen G. White, *Life Sketches*, p. 196.